Octavia

Social Reformer and Co-Founder of the National Trust

Foreword
by Dame Fiona Reynolds
Director-General, National Trust

In the run-up to the centenary of Octavia Hill's death, the National Trust recruited its four millionth member. Proof, if any were needed, that the cause she passionately promoted remains as relevant now as it was in 1912.

The National Trust is perhaps the most enduring of Octavia Hill's achievements. It is thanks to her determination that so many beautiful places – coast, countryside, great houses, vernacular buildings and much more – have been saved and are available for millions to enjoy. But as this book makes clear, her interests were wide and her achievements many. All her activities stemmed from her deeply held view that everyone's life should be enriched by beauty.

Expansion of over-crowded cities, rampant industrialisation and untrammelled pursuit of profit were the prevailing forces of her time. Her beliefs – in beauty, in history, in the importance of fresh air and places to roam, and in well-designed, well-managed places to live – were ahead of their time.

Octavia Hill was both a visionary and a pragmatist. Indeed, she spent most of her life putting her ideas into practice. Her work led directly to the creation of the National Trust, the public housing movement and the recognition of the importance of providing green, open spaces in towns and cities. All are central to our quality of life today.

This book explores Octavia Hill's life, from her early influences to her all-important relationship with John Ruskin; from her pioneering housing work to her involvement with the conservation movement and the foundation of the National Trust. Her energy, determination and focus on improving lives through access to beauty, nature and history are striking. But for her life and work we would all be the poorer today. This book is a fitting and timely tribute to a most remarkable woman.

Octavia Hill, 1838–1912
by Peter Clayton

'Octavia Hill's was an exemplary life of personal service to the highest interests of the nation,' wrote an obituarist. She was one of only three women invited in their own right to Queen Victoria's Golden Jubilee service at Westminster Abbey in 1887. Clever, brave and resolute, she worked tirelessly for over 50 years towards her vision of a socially inclusive society 'for ever, for everyone'. Her methods of personal, friendly, hands-on management of rented properties successfully redeemed slum areas and promoted healthy communities. She showed how access to the arts and beauty in the form of open spaces and historic places could help heal what Benjamin Disraeli called the 'Two Nations' class divide.

Octavia Hill has never been easy to classify. 'She was,' wrote a contemporary, 'something akin to an English government department and a seaside lodging house landlady.' 'She combined,' wrote another, 'the poetical with the practical.' Although short of stature, and habitually dowdy in her dress, her commanding personality and obvious intellect, along with piercing eyes, made her a formidable presence. Her achievements came from her clear-eyed vision and a unique combination of personal qualities that inspired loyalty and respect in people from all walks of life.

In this book we record her substantial legacy. Today she is remembered primarily as a founder of the National Trust. Others know her as the 'Florence Nightingale of housing' who created the profession of housing management. She pioneered the modern concepts of social work, housing associations, civic societies, the National Trust, the Army Cadet movement and the green belt around London. But just to catalogue single aspects of her work is to underestimate the comprehensive nature of her vision. For her, individual and family happiness derived from not one but many sources. Good housing and recreational open space were just two of them. Education was another. Like the Victorian art and social critic John Ruskin, she was primarily a teacher who throughout her life created models for others to emulate. Hers was a vision of a society of independent, responsible and mutually supportive individuals.

▲ Octavia Hill's portrait by John Singer Sargent, now in the National Portrait Gallery, was commissioned by friends and gifted to her on her 60th birthday. Commenting on the portrait, Octavia's companion Harriot Yorke said, 'Octavia never looked sideways.'

▲ An artist's impression of the Birthplace House on the South Brink, Wisbech, 1811.

▶ Octavia Hill's Birthplace House today. Built for the Vavazor family around 1740, it is a Grade II* listed building. The Education Centre includes a library and archive. The garden is open to the public and features a memorial to victims of cholera by the Cardozo Kindersley Workshop, Cambridge.

Although she made it clear that there were no codified Octavia Hill certainties to be handed down to future generations, her ideas and the issues she identified have a strong resonance today. The displays and educational activities in her Birthplace House in Wisbech, Cambridgeshire, celebrate both her life and today's organisations that grew from her work. In the spirit of Octavia Hill, it is staffed by volunteers and a percentage of the proceeds from the sale of this book will go to the Octavia Hill Birthplace Museum Trust.

The Hill Family

'I am your Disciple.'
Octavia Hill, aged 40, writing to her mother

Octavia Hill's father, James Hill, was a banker. He had come to Wisbech from Peterborough in 1818 and married Ann Jecks, daughter of a wealthy timber merchant.

The Hill family's substantial early 18th-century family house, now 7 and 8 South Brink and Grade II* listed, remains one of the finest buildings in the town. But in 1825 a large crowd gathered outside to read a notice on the railings beginning 'Truly sorry ...'. It announced that the bank was in difficulties. A national banking crisis had destroyed over a hundred provincial banks including James Hill's. Farmer John Peck wrote in his diary: 'Attended the examination of Mr Hill, a bankrupt. Although a loser, I really could not help feeling hurt at his distress.' However, a dividend was paid and James re-established himself as an apparently prosperous corn merchant.

Hill was an idealistic businessman who refused to eat sugar because it was the product of slave labour. He once rode to Cambridge to save the life of a man sentenced to death for sheep stealing.

◄ *James Hill, Octavia's father.*

His experiences during the crisis of 1825 at the mercy of the 'imperfect monetary system' radicalised him further. He began to agitate for the reform of society.

When Ann died, James Hill married her sister, Eliza. She died in 1832, leaving him a widower with six children. Then, in 1835, James married Caroline Southwood Smith; he is said to have read her anonymous article on education and, after discovering who the author was, offered her the post of governess to his children. She was to bear him a further five children: Miranda, Gertrude, Octavia, Emily and Florence. Miranda wrote of her mother: 'Her children learnt from infancy that if a thing was right it must be done.'

◄ *Caroline Hill, Octavia's mother.*

Dr Thomas Southwood Smith

'Ages shall honour, in their hearts enshrined / Thee, Southwood Smith, Physician of Mankind / Bringer of Air, Light, Health into the home / Of the rich poor of happier years to come.'
Leigh Hunt, poet, essayist, critic (1784–1859)

Dr Thomas Southwood Smith (1788–1861), Octavia Hill's maternal grandfather, was a champion of rights for the poor. The Hill family derived much of their knowledge and abhorrence of the injustice and inequality of existing society from him.

Southwood Smith had been the prime mover of the Anatomy Act of 1832. He argued that unless a legal supply of bodies for dissection was allowed to surgeons, they could only acquire skill by operating on the living bodies of the poor. As Physician to the London Fever Hospital during the cholera outbreaks of the 1840s, he had little doubt that the high mortality rates in the poorest areas of London originated in the appalling sanitary conditions that he had seen. He took the Marquess of Normanby (the Home Secretary) and Lord Shaftesbury to Bethnal Green where there were open cesspits and streets 'wholly without drainage'. In such conditions fever was endemic. Southwood Smith told them, 'The annual slaughter is by causes that are preventable ... 126 persons perish every day in England alone, whose lives might be saved ... the effect is the same as 20 or 30 thousand of them were annually taken from their homes and put to death.'

Watercolourist Margaret Gillies (1803–87), one of the first independent women artists, lived with Dr Southwood Smith. She went down into the coal mines to draw attention to the conditions of the women and children who worked there. Her sketches formed part of the first illustrated government report and were probably decisive in promoting reform. Young Octavia wished to become an artist herself.

It was at a dinner party at Southwood Smith's home that James Hill met Robert Owen, the man who offered a remedy for society's malaise.

▶ *Portrait of Octavia's grandfather, Dr Thomas Southwood Smith, by his partner, Margaret Gillies.*

▶ *Octavia Hill (top left) and her sisters: Miranda (centre); Florence (top right); Emily (bottom right); Gertrude (bottom left).*

Towards a New Moral World

'Society may be formed so as to exist without crime, without poverty, with health greatly improved and with happiness improved a hundredfold.'
Robert Owen, *A New View of Society*

Cotton mill proprietor Robert Owen (1771–1858) believed that all human beings were essentially good. Environment, which included not only their physical surroundings but also the social conditions in which they were raised as children, corrupted them, not original sin. At New Lanark in Scotland, he created for his mill workers a model industrial community, which led him to campaign for a world 'free of competition, poverty, crime and misery'. He believed a 'New Moral World' would emerge from mutual cooperation, a benign physical environment and an effective secular education programme. In a memorial to Owen, members of the Society for Promoting National Regeneration wrote: 'You came amongst us as a rich man amongst the poor but did not call us rabble ... or with a sneer on your lips, no covert scorn in the tone of your voice ....'

For James Hill, Owen's ideas were a compelling alternative to the prevailing corruption of society. Hill started Wisbech's first

▲ *New Lanark Mill, where Robert Owen's management style based on cooperation and harmony inspired his work towards a 'New Moral World'.*

newspaper, *The Star in the East*, 'to help forward the cause of humanity' by propagating Owen's ideas. He wrote much of the newspaper himself in a distinctive polemical style, attacking state institutions, local personalities and self-interest groups. He made enemies, and hostility focused on his Wisbech Infant School.

Figures of Robert Owen (left) and Jeremy Bentham on display in the Birthplace House. The one of Bentham is a replica of the auto-icon in University College, London.

Jeremy Bentham (1748–1832)

Jeremy Bentham, an associate of Dr Southwood Smith, was a social and legal reformer who proposed a world where happiness could be achieved by allowing individuals the freedom to do as they wished.

A Southwood Smith article – 'Use of the Dead to the Living' – led to the Anatomy Act of 1832, ending the trafficking in bodies for anatomical schools. Bentham shared Southwood Smith's interest in reforming the system. When Bentham died he left instructions for the public dissection of his own body and its preservation as an 'auto-icon'. He entrusted the task to Dr Southwood Smith, who dressed the skeleton in Bentham's everyday clothes and used Bentham's hair to cover the wax head of the effigy. In 1850, Southwood Smith gave the auto-icon to University College, London, where the original is displayed.

Wisbech Infant School

'We'll try if we can help to mould, / A world of other stuff'
Inscription above the door of Wisbech Infant School,
adapted from William Wordsworth's *Rob Roy's Grave*

In July 1838 James and Caroline Hill opened Wisbech Infant School as 'a service to the wretched poor' in a small, purpose-built Greek-style building which quietly expressed its nobility of purpose. Today it forms the foyer of the town's Angles Theatre. *The Star in the East* announced that the school was to be 'a place where cleanliness, cheerfulness and kindness preside: where they [the children] will breathe the purer air than that of the alleys and canal banks and where, removed from the sight of vulgarity and vice, the faculties with which nature has endowed them shall be allowed and aided to expand in natural beauty'.

The teaching methods were distinctive and controversial. According to Octavia Hill, her mother was the first woman in England to use the Pestalozzian system in England. For Swiss educational reformer Johann Pestalozzi (1746–1827), the purpose of education was not to promote the habits 'of blind obedience and of prescribed diligence, but a preparation for independent action'. In *The Star in the East* Caroline Hill wrote, 'The tender minds of infants can only receive a certain quantity: we take so much pains to cram them with errors

▲ The Angles Theatre, Wisbech, originally Wisbech Infant School, is the third oldest theatre in the country.

▼ The Star in the East *report about an event at Wisbech Infant School, founded and run by James and Caroline Hill.*

◄ Blue plaque on the Angles Theatre.

that nature's beautiful activity is checked. The infant becomes the passive recipient of false impressions and the man becomes an imperfect being.' Children were allowed to develop at their own pace with few formal lessons. This contrasted with the prevailing monitorial system, where learning was by rote and designed to produce obedient children with a limited range of skills. No religion was taught at the school, merely 'the importance of truth, justice and mutual kindness and forbearance'. To its enemies it became 'The Infidel School'.

Paradise Postponed

'Equal rights are our aim, / Cooperation our plan, / To labour be ready, / Always be steady, / And we shall be happy again and again.'
From the 'Social Workman's Song'

Contact with the parents of poor children led the Hills to open Wisbech Infant School in the evenings as a 'Hall for the People'. The 'Mental Improvement Society' held meetings and lectures, and members contributed weekly to the United Advancement Society fund to buy land and emancipate them. A co-operative store sold goods at cost, to the anger of local traders. Evening activities in the Hall for the People involved dancing and singing, including the 'Social Workman's Song', sung to the tune of 'Hearts of Oak'.

Caroline Hill wrote in a memoir that by the time Octavia Hill was born on 3 December 1838, 'the storm clouds were gathering thick and fast' on their house. By early 1840, James Hill was bankrupt for a second time. His assets were sold and the family left Wisbech. The next decade was one of hardship.

▲ A hand-coloured print of Queen Victoria's Coronation Feast which took place in Wisbech Market Place in 1838, the year in which Octavia Hill was born.

▼ The Manea Colony was a short-lived attempt to create a new society on a farm, 10 miles (16kms) from Wisbech.

Manea Colony

William Hodson, a parent of one of the schoolchildren, established an Owenite colony in the Cambridgeshire parish of Manea, which generated further local opposition. A prospectus for the Manea Colony promised 'A union of the working classes ... with no distinction ... no individual property. All will labour for the benefit of the whole ... all will be equal.'

Idyllic Finchley

'There is nothing which cannot be achieved by means of affection. Love is the means.'
Caroline Hill

The family lived first in a cottage in Epping, Essex, provided by Caroline's father, Dr Thomas Southwood Smith. There Emily was born, James and Caroline's fourth child. Southwood Smith and Margaret Gillies supported the family, and took Gertrude, Octavia's older sister, to live with them. Later the Hill family moved to Leeds, a fast-growing town and centre of radical activity, where Florence was born, the last of James and Caroline's five daughters.

According to his wife's memoir, James Hill suffered 'a temporary fit of insanity' and by the mid 1840s they had parted. We know little of the last 30 years of his life. He is a shadowy presence in Hill family affairs, dying in the home of Margaret (one of his daughters from an earlier marriage) in 1872; he was buried in Highgate Cemetery in north London. Long after his death, Caroline wrote of James, 'He had genius ... and immense business talent, industry and energy, almost superhuman. A man of large, liberal and friendly kind spirit who would not willingly have injured anyone, but on the contrary would have done good to all.'

By 1846, Caroline and her daughters had settled in Brownswell Cottage in rural Finchley, to the north of London. Octavia and her sisters spent an idyllic stress-free childhood, mostly outdoors, 'leaping ditches and climbing trees'. Octavia's earliest recorded words were: 'Mummy, I wish I could have a field so large I could run in it forever.'

▲ Leaping Ditches and Climbing Trees *by Mari L'Anson depicts Octavia's idyllic childhood years in Finchley.*

▲ *At Octavia Hill's Birthplace House are displays linked to the cultural circles in which the Hill family moved.* Haymaking at Highgate *by George Downes is a recreation of a lost painting by Margaret Gillies. It is thought to show an event she experienced as a child at Hampstead Heath when children's author Hans Christian Andersen came to visit.*

Caroline's educational theories were now practised exclusively on her daughters. She was not a disciplinarian. Real study, she thought, should not be undertaken until the child was about 15 years old. What Octavia called Caroline's 'keen insight into the working of a child's mind' meant that many learning processes became games, such as teaching imaginary schoolchildren.

Margaret Howitt, a childhood friend, said Octavia was an 'ardent, eager child, with a quick sense of the ludicrous ... hidden under a precise determined manner.' Although not the oldest sister, Octavia was the born leader.

The Ladies Guild

'Women should have pecuniary resources; the whole burden of the maintenance of society need not necessarily rest, as now, on men ... There are many women who would be glad to meet with remunerative occupation.'
Caroline Hill, in a letter to *The Illustrated London News*, 1851

In 1851, Caroline Hill moved into London to manage the Ladies Guild, a Christian Socialist cooperative venture. Ten years after the Wisbech debacle Caroline wrote to Robert Owen to commend the new venture as an 'association of women of the educated class, combined to conduct certain works for their pecuniary benefit'.

The Guild was financed by barrister Edward Vansittart Neale (1810–92), a nephew of William Wilberforce. 'Cooperation,' said Neale, 'is aimed at constructing a society ruled by fellowship and mutual trust where man can develop his physical and spiritual powers to the full.' He eventually lost £60,000 backing cooperative enterprises.

When Octavia was aged 14, her mother put her in charge of the workroom at the Guild, and the Ragged School girls who worked there, painting and decorating glass tables. On her first day Octavia characteristically went over to a 'List of Rules' pinned to the wall, read them and tore them down. All her work was to be based not on rules which treat people collectively, but on a separate unique relationship with each individual, responsive to his or her strengths and weaknesses, needs and aspirations.

At this time she acquired her impatience with those who dabbled in 'good works'. She wrote: 'I don't know what there is in the word "lady" which will connect itself with all kinds of things I despise and hate; first and most universally it suggests a want of perseverance and bending before small obstacles, a continual "I would if ..."'.' She had a life-long distaste for unfocused 'promiscuous charity'. For her, friendship and care were as important as money.

▲ The Great Exhibition of 1851, at which the Ladies Guild exhibited painted glass tables.

▶ This display in Octavia Hill's Birthplace House depicts Prince Albert's 'model dwellings for families' which originated from the work of Dr Thomas Southwood Smith. The actual building was originally shown at the Great Exhibition of 1851 and is today in Kennington Park, south-east London, as Prince Consort Lodge.

The Christian Socialists

'Do noble things, not dream them.'
From Charles Kingsley's 'A Farewell', and often quoted by Octavia Hill

In 1848, the great Chartist demonstration on Kennington Common, south London, prompted a group of Christians to establish a non-political social reform agenda. Their inspiration was Frederick Denison Maurice (1805–72), a clergyman and theologian, who advocated Christian action to change society and eradicate poverty. 'Competition is put forth as the law of the universe. That is a lie. The time is come for us to declare that it is a lie, by word and deed,' he said.

For three years, young Octavia went regularly to hear Maurice preach in Lincoln's Inn Chapel. He believed that the root of all evil was mankind's ignorance of God, and advocated social action by individuals to restore the health of society. The aim was to bridge the gulf between the 'unchristian socialists and the unsocialist

▲ *Frederick Denison Maurice, who inspired the Christian Socialist movement.*

◀ *A boy chimney sweep on display in Octavia's Birthplace House, inspired by Charles Kingsley's* The Water Babies, *a book that popularised Maurice's ideas. Kingsley regularly addressed meetings at the Hall of Association, near the Ladies Guild.*

Christians'. As a result of Maurice's preaching, in 1857 Octavia was confirmed into the Church of England at Christ Church in Marylebone.

It was around this time that Octavia became secretary to the women's classes at the new Working Men's College which had been started by the Christian Socialists. Her faith was profound, enduring and remarkably unsectarian. It animated her work throughout her life. It was quiet and undemonstrative; she appears to have rarely mentioned God, except in letters to close friends. For Octavia Hill actions, not words, were the expression of her belief.

11

John Ruskin

'Let us reform our schools, and we shall find little need of reform in our prisons.'
John Ruskin (1819–1900)

▲ *John Ruskin, who encouraged Octavia Hill's artistic talent and financed her early housing experiments.*

In 1853, John Ruskin visited the Ladies Guild. He was already celebrated as the author of *Modern Painters*, written to defend the landscape artist J.M.W. Turner (1775–1851). Ruskin's *Stones of Venice* had documented the buildings of a city in decline; he had drawn the Casa D'Oro as the workmen 'were hammering it down before my face', and declared that 'the rate at which Venice is going is about that of a lump of sugar in hot tea'. For Ruskin there were sermons in the stones of Venice. Great cities and civilisations would decline if their ethical foundations crumbled. He began to see what he called the 'storm-clouds of the 19th century' gathering over London.

Ruskin was charmed by the Hill family of young articulate women. For the next decade Octavia trained with him as an art copyist. In 1863, the Society of Antiquaries commissioned her to undertake work for them. But, as Octavia put it, 'Ruskin showed me something else I would rather do than paint like Leonardo.' During their long conversations Ruskin expressed his concern at what he saw as the absence of social relations between the classes that threatened the very fabric of society. Octavia spoke of 'the frightful want of feeling in all classes' but 'thought that rich people were now waking up to a sense of their duties'. 'Yes,' said Ruskin, '... I think we may live to see some great changes in society.'

There is little doubt that Octavia became Ruskin's reporter on the miseries of London life. She was dealing daily with children who endured lives of almost unimaginable deprivation and poverty. She had once gone in search of a child who had failed to come to work and had seen her bleak, desolate home. Poor people were socially alienated and geographically isolated in ramshackle, overcrowded slums. The needs of simple sustenance and survival dominated their lives.

▶ *Octavia Hill painted this copy of the 1501 Portrait of Doge Leonardo Loredan by Giovanni Bellini; the original hangs in the National Gallery, London, and this copy is in the Ruskin Collection held by Museums Sheffield.*

Face-to-Face with Poverty

'There is no wealth but life ...'
John Ruskin, *Unto this Last* (1860)

For Ruskin the appalling physical condition and spiritual enervation of much of the population were an affront to a supposed civilisation. He saw all around him on the streets people suffering 'diminished lives in the midst of noise, of darkness, and of deadly exhalation'. Similarly, for Octavia the first-hand experience of poverty had been a great shock: 'I was plunged into these new conditions from our homely little cottage and garden in Finchley into a tall, rather dark house in an unlovely street ... from the wonderful freedom of outdoor life and friendly relationships with neighbours, to the constraint which was necessary when streets were ill-lighted and inadequately policed ... I watched through the great windows, the London poor pass in rain and fog ... I sat and cried ... at the remembrance of Tottenham Court Road on Saturday night with its haggard faces. There the first awful wonder about why evil was permitted came to me.'

▼ *The Workhouse in Southwell, Nottinghamshire, now a National Trust property. The Poor Law Amendment Act of 1834 created the workhouses that dominated the Victorian response to poverty.*

The Poor Laws provided the ultimate refuge in the workhouse. Other community responses involved ad hoc charity such as soup kitchens. National leaders were content to allow market forces to determine the common good. The struggle for survival was beneficial, they argued; every individual should have the utmost freedom to pursue his own interests. Any interference in this natural mechanism could only damage the rights of property. These were regarded as sacrosanct.

In his essays comprising *Unto this Last*, Ruskin launched a full assault on Society's complacency: 'That country is the richest which nourishes the greatest numbers of noble and happy human beings; that man is richest, who, having perfected the functions of his own life to the utmost, has also the widest helpful influence, both personal, and by means of his possessions, over the lives of others.' Ruskin concluded that people, not buildings, are a nation's capital. He shocked readers of the *Pall Mall Gazette* by criticising the conventional business ethics of the day, saying, 'The rich not only refuse food to the poor; they refuse wisdom; they refuse virtue; they refuse salvation.'

▲▼ *Cushions on display in the Birthplace House, featuring phrases from Ruskin's* Unto This Last *which challenged the values of Victorian society.*

The Birth of Social Housing

'A greater power is in the hands of the landlords and landladies than that of school-teachers – power either of life or death, physical and spiritual.'
Octavia Hill, *Homes of the London Poor*, 1875

When John Ruskin inherited an income of £4,000 a year, he asked Octavia what she would do in his position. 'Something to provide better homes for the poor,' she replied. She had walked beneath a narrow arch near her home behind Marylebone High Street into Paradise Place, also known as 'Little Hell' (now Garbutt Place, where today a commemorative plaque to Octavia is on one

▲ Inside Paradise Place. This reconstruction in Octavia Hill's Birthplace House, based on contemporary illustrations and accounts, shows a family living in damp, cramped conditions as the landlord collects the rent.

◂ A model of Paradise Place as Octavia would first have seen it. The 1861 census showed 37 people living in just eight rooms.

of the houses). Ruskin bought three houses here and handed over management to Octavia. 'More awful abodes of human beings I never entered,' wrote Octavia to her sister. It was a parallel universe unknown to the wealthy residents of the big houses in the streets of London's wealthiest parish, who generated the casual labour that their unseen neighbours in Paradise Place depended upon.

Octavia became the friendly face of 'landlordism'. She personally collected the rents and used the weekly transaction as an opportunity to take an interest in the tenants' lives, establishing community cohesion. Her methods were firm but compassionate: she patiently fostered a reciprocal respect between landlord and tenant; she expected tenants to pay the rent. 'When I began collecting rents I was told it was impossible for the very poor to pay regularly,' she said, 'but from the first I insisted on weekly payments

▶ St Christopher's Buildings, St Christopher's Place, off London's Oxford Street. Originally Barretts Court, it was renamed by Octavia after her favourite saint. The bas relief, based on a Dürer print, is by William Morris.

and the money was found.' The landlord provided an efficient service in return.

Octavia's style was managerial but not dictatorial. She and her trained 'fellow workers' (the cooperative movement term she always used when referring to her colleagues, whether workers or donors) relied on routine attention to the detailed needs of buildings and tenants. Her idea was to 'improve the people and the buildings together'. She would not go into a tenant's home without being invited and refused to show visitors the homes of her tenants, insisting on 'perfect strictness in our business relations, perfect respectfulness in personal relations'. And she always pointed out that she learned as much from her tenants as they learned from her: 'Their energy and hope amid overwhelming difficulties have made me ashamed of my own laziness and despair.'

Victorian attitudes to the poor were often dismissive. 'Where are the poor to live?' Octavia asked a landlord's agent. 'I don't know,' he replied. 'But they must keep off the St John's Wood Estate.'

The common assumption amongst property owners was that it was impossible to let property to the poor because they would destroy it. Those who owned slum properties did so either by the chance of inheritance, or were knowingly – or unknowingly – exploitative. One funeral director told Octavia, 'Yes, Miss; of course there are plenty of bad debts. It's not the rents I look to but the deaths I get out of the houses.' On two other Marylebone sites – Freshwater Place and Barretts Court – the Paradise Place experiment was successfully repeated as she gained other investors.

Octavia profiled her work as business, not charity, and attracted more investors who were willing to buy houses and accept only a 5 per cent return on capital instead of the possible 12 per cent ('safe as houses') achievable by overcrowding. Volunteers were the mainstay of her work. Once trained by her they often went on to operate independently elsewhere for other owners. Even Princess Alice, daughter of Queen Victoria, visited incognito to see Octavia's methods at first hand and began similar work in Germany.

The management methods balanced the interests of the landlord, the tenants – who were 'so sorted as to be helpful to one another' – and the building itself, which was routinely maintained and repaired; whatever money remained was spent on additional amenities in consultation with the tenants. Fundamental to this, of course, was Octavia's insistence on payment of rent. By 1874 Octavia and her fellow workers controlled over 3,000 tenancies on 17 sites around London.

The birth of social inclusion

In Paradise Place, Octavia Hill and John Ruskin established the modern concepts of ethical investment and social housing, and demonstrated that a root cause of society's malaise was the complete absence of understanding or contact between the classes. The better-off owed a duty of care to the poor – not just because it was right, but also because it was prudent not to let any section of society be marginalised or ignored. The birth of social housing was also the birth of social inclusion.

◀ Princess Alice, daughter of Queen Victoria, bequeathed this cross to Octavia Hill in her will. The Princess translated Octavia's book Homes of the London Poor into German.

The Kyrle Society

'There are two great wants in the life of the poor of our large towns ... the want of space, and the want of beauty.'
Octavia Hill

Founded by Octavia Hill and her sister Miranda by 1877, the Kyrle Society was named after philanthropist John Kyrle (1637–1724) from Ross-on-Wye in Herefordshire. Alexander Pope's exemplar featured in one of Kyrle's Moral Essays on 'The Use of Riches', and Kyrle spent much of his fortune improving his community.

Octavia realised that the great burden of the poor was 'not just poverty but ugliness'. To supply material needs was essential, but if life were bereft of beauty its value was considerably diminished.

▲ This window by Hazel Parry in Octavia Hill's Birthplace House commemorates the work of the Kyrle Society. It depicts Octavia (top left) and artist William Morris (top right), who spoke at the first Kyrle Society meeting of the need to work 'to the utmost of our power to achieve its ends'.

A letter to The Times

Octavia was adept at drawing attention to her work. Many years after the formation of the Kyrle Society, Octavia wrote an appeal to *The Times* newspaper, which began:

Sir

May we beg a small portion of your space to bring the needs and the claims of the Kyrle Society before your readers?

For nearly 30 years the Society has pursued its objects, its work increasing readily and steadily. There is scarcely any important open space which has been secured for the public during that time with the acquisition of which it has not been connected. Help has been given to poor libraries of all kinds (other than rate-aided) by the literature distribution branch, grants of books having been sent not only all over England, but to the Shetland Islands, the West Indies and even Australia.

The oratorios and concerts given by the choir and the musical branch have given pleasure to thousands of the poorer members of the metropolitan community; while the decorative branch has transformed numerous bare and ugly parish halls, club-rooms, and similar institutions into bright, artistic, and pleasant places of rest and recreation ....

The Kyrle Society and its 13 provincial imitators were societies 'For the Diffusion of Beauty'. Members aimed to bring 'beauty to the people'. This groundbreaking organisation's music, open space and literature committees introduced 'colour, space and music' into the environment of Victorian cities; this union of concerned, committed volunteers and supporters later became a prototype for the National Trust.

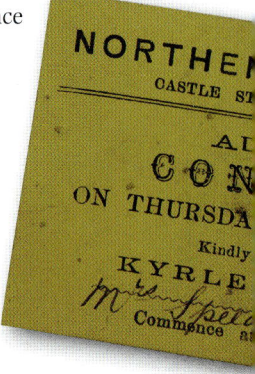

▶ A concert ticket for a musical event organised by the Kyrle Society in 1877. Music was one of the beauties of life that the Society believed everyone should have the chance to enjoy.

Open Spaces

'Places to sit in, places to play in, places to stroll in, and places to spend the day in.'
Octavia Hill, *Homes of the London Poor*, 1875

As London grew without planning controls it engulfed fields and filled in remaining urban recreational space. At Freshwater Place, the second Marylebone property that Octavia managed, she had cleared a rubbish-strewn courtyard and created a playground with trees. She believed that a garden should be the complement of every home and that play space and 'the healthy gift of air and the joy of plants and flowers' were vital in everyone's life. Large open spaces accessible to all were also essential.

The first of Octavia's great battles was to prevent building on Swiss Cottage Fields, just north of Regent's Park, where she had taken the children of tenants to play. Around this time she became engaged to one of her colleagues, Edward Bond (who later became an MP); it appears that his mother did not approve of the union, and the engagement was broken.

Following this, her failure to save Swiss Cottage Fields, and a public quarrel and final rift with Ruskin when she failed to support his plans for a Colony

▲ A topical 1883 *Punch* cartoon, quoting Octavia Hill on the 'value of small open spaces' and depicting children playing near their homes.

▲ One of Octavia's open spaces is Postman's Park in London, where memorials 'To Heroic Self Sacrifice' include this tribute to Alice Ayres, whose death at the age of 26 caused much public interest. She was also commemorated in a mural in Red Cross Hall, founded by Octavia Hill.

outside Sheffield, Octavia suffered a breakdown and began three years of rest and travel. During this period, Harriot Yorke became Octavia's companion and took on much of the detailed work that was causing her stress. Octavia's family and fellow workers continued the housing work in her absence. The delegation necessitated by her ill health fostered independent action by her workers and enabled her methods to be replicated elsewhere.

On her return to health, Octavia's focus shifted. She became a doughty fighter in the open space movement, sitting on committees, making speeches, helping to save even the smallest neighbourhood open space as an 'outdoor sitting room'. Throughout the 1880s and 1890s her campaigns on behalf of 'pure earth, clean air and blue sky' led to the creation and retention of numerous urban and national open spaces, including London's Parliament Hill Fields, Vauxhall Park and Hilly Fields.

17

Red Cross Garden

'And the wilderness shall blossom as the rose'
Ceramic inscription on the wall of Red Cross Garden, from Isaiah 35:1

In 1884 Octavia became manager of some Ecclesiastical Commissioners properties in Southwark, south of London Bridge. They had replaced small cottages and their tiny back yards with large block dwellings. Octavia persuaded the Commissioners to provide some recreational space as an essential amenity. They leased her a tiny scrap of ground, anciently called Red Cross after a burial site. Here in the heart of extreme deprivation the Kyrle Society created a garden with formal flowerbeds, a bandstand, mosaics, a covered play area and an ornamental pond. It was 'a large open-air sitting room for the young and the old who lived in the numerous courts in the neighbourhood ...'.

Solicitor Robert Hunter, an old ally and the legal advisor to the Commons and Footpath Preservation Society, donated goldfish; Hardwicke Rawnsley, who had collected rents for Octavia as a young man and was now a clergyman in the Lake District, wrote a sonnet to celebrate its opening by the Archbishop of Canterbury. Hunter became a trustee of the site. A few years later, both Hunter and Rawnsley were to be founders, with Octavia, of the National Trust.

▲ *An artist's impression of opening day at Red Cross Garden, Hall and Cottages.*

The bandstand and mosaics expressed Octavia's determination to bring high-quality art in all its forms into the lives of people living in squalor. Despite dire predictions of vandalism and many 'rough characters and boisterous boys in the area', Octavia was able to report that 'the order has been excellent; there has hardly been a flower plucked'.

Six pretty cottages and an elegant community hall overlook the garden, which was restored to its Victorian glory and reopened in 2005 with the help of a Heritage Lottery Fund (HLF) grant. Today, more than 125 years after its creation, the core elements of Octavia Hill's pioneering work for healthy cities are evident in the design: attractive, well-built dwellings, a community garden and a community meeting place.

▲ *Red Cross Garden, photographed in 1900.*

▶ *Red Cross Garden today, now run by Bankside Open Spaces Trust. Octavia Housing owns the cottages.*

Red Cross Hall

'A bright drawing room for the neighbourhood ...'
Octavia Hill

Architect Elijah Hoole (1837–1912), who designed the cottages overlooking Red Cross Garden, created alongside them the elegant hammer-beamed Red Cross Hall. Like the Hall for the People in Wisbech 50 years earlier, it offered warmth, comfort and informal activities. Young Elizabeth Casson (1881–1954), who later became a doctor and founder of the first school of Occupational Therapy in England, was in charge of the formal entertainments. Octavia wrote: 'When one turns in from the mud, fog and general dinginess of a London winter afternoon in Southwark, tea, coffee, warm drinks, cakes and oranges are sold and the Hall becomes a bright drawing room for the neighbourhood and pleasant groups congregate at various tables and look at illustrated papers and books.'

Red Cross Hall became a centre for progressive social reform. From 1887, the executive committee of the new Women's University Settlement met there. Academic interest in Octavia's proven method of social outreach grew. After the foundation in 1895 of the London School of Economics, Octavia cooperated with the embryonic School of Sociology, which developed professional social work.

Together, Red Cross Hall, Cottages and Garden comprise a landmark urban development, expressing the interdependence of housing, open space and indoor community meeting place. The venture anticipated some of the core precepts of town planning by several years. The Metropolitan Public Gardens Association annual report of 1918 referred to it as 'A miniature Garden Village in the heart of the inner city'.

◄ Murals by Walter Crane commemorating extraordinary acts of bravery decorated Red Cross Hall. This one, recreated by Dan Dunton, depicts local girl Alice Ayres who rescued three children from a fire, before falling to her death.

► Army Cadet figure: Octavia Hill formed the first independent battalion in London for boys who lived in Southwark.

Army Cadet movement

The modern Army Cadet movement began in Red Cross Hall. The inaugural meeting of the Southwark Corps of the Army Cadet Force was held in 1889. It was established by Octavia Hill to provide for 'our Southwark lads ... exercise, discipline and obedience ... the very best possible education'. Essentially a social inclusion exercise, it took into its ranks only genuine working boys; two years later they were marching in the Lord Mayor's Show. Octavia became their Honorary Colonel. One of the officers said: 'When she took the chair at our meetings ... I would compare her to Queen Elizabeth ... she displayed all the great queen's resolution, power of command ... and scrupulous reckoning of every half-penny.'

The National Trust
For Ever, For Everyone

'Mark my words, Miss Hill, this is going to be a very big thing.'
The Duke of Westminster, on the founding of the National Trust in 1895

Throughout the 1880s and 1890s, Octavia Hill led campaigns to secure urban recreational open spaces for posterity. In addition to major sites such as Hilly Fields, Vauxhall Park and Parliament Hill Fields, she helped save numerous smaller neighbourhood sites in London as 'outdoor sitting rooms'. Some featured buildings such as the Geffrye Almshouses in Shoreditch and the Trinity Almshouses in the Mile End Road.

However, Octavia Hill and Robert Hunter were aware that none of these hard-won or generously donated public amenities was truly secure. There was no legally appointed body capable of holding land or buildings 'for ever, for everyone'; they could be sold or diminished at any time by their owners for short-term gain.

As early as 1884, Hunter proposed to the National Health Society a 'benevolent rather than a commercial body for accepting, holding and purchasing' land. A few years later the idea was taken up by Hardwicke Rawnsley, a friend of Ruskin and now vicar of Crosthwaite, Cumbria. By this time Ruskin was living at Brantwood, his home in the Lake District. The whole beauty of the Lake District had been threatened with municipal and railway company depredations. Even the celebrated Poet's Stone, bearing the inscriptions of Samuel Taylor Coleridge and the Wordsworths, had been destroyed. Rawnsley, a formidable campaigner, became Chairman of the Lake District Defence Society and, in 1895, with Octavia and Hunter, became one of the three founders of the new 'National Trust for Historic Sites and Natural Scenery'. The name was proposed by Hunter; Octavia's suggestion had been the 'Commons and Gardens Trust'. It was ultimately registered as The National Trust for Places of Historic Interest or Natural Beauty. Both Octavia and Hunter were experienced in private and parliamentary lobbying, and he wrote the Act of Parliament that enabled the Trust to hold land in perpetuity – as its motto says, 'For Ever, For Everyone'.

▲ *The Centenary Mural in Octavia Hill's Birthplace House features over one hundred National Trust properties. The characters on the right – standing on the Giant's Causeway in Northern Ireland, now in the care of the Trust – portray those whose ideas were central to the Trust's founding, amongst them Thomas Southwood Smith, John Ruskin, Robert Owen, F.D. Maurice, Thomas Carlyle and John Kyrle.*

▲ *Dinas Oleu in Wales, the very first National Trust property.*

Octavia Hill's special contribution was an established network of donors and volunteers who gave 'gifts of money or gifts of time'. Their numbers included the Duke of Westminster, who had been a leader on the provision of artisan housing on his 600-acre (242-ha) London estate. He agreed to become President of the Trust and an active member of the Executive Committee.

Early properties acquired by the new Trust set the template for the future: they were an eclectic mix of heritage, history, conservation and landscape beauty. The first, acquired on 16 October 1894, was the Barmouth Bay headland Dinas Oleu ('fortress of light') in west Wales. The donor was Mrs Fanny Talbot, a wealthy philanthropist and friend of Ruskin. The purchase by Octavia Hill of the second property, the 14th-century Alfriston Priest's House (now Alfriston Clergy House) in East Sussex, for £10, flagged up the romantic transcendentalist principle whereby, as Octavia put it, 'places become enriched by the life that has been passed in them'. The acquisition of the first 2 acres (0.8ha) of the surviving 800-acre (323-ha) undrained Wicken Fen in Cambridgeshire pioneered the idea of nature conservation.

For many years the National Trust did not buy any large houses following an unhappy experience with Barrington Court in Somerset. Purchased when it had deteriorated to such an extent that it was little more than a cattle barn, the cost of repairs spiralled. Harriot Yorke, Octavia's companion, was inclined to intone 'Remember Barrington' when proposals were made to acquire larger buildings, and obstructed such propositions until her death in 1930.

▲ *The 14th-century Alfriston Clergy House, purchased by the National Trust when it was a ruin and the first building to come into its ownership.*

▲ *Carlyle's House in Cheyne Row, Chelsea, acquired by the National Trust in 1936. Scottish writer Thomas Carlyle was a major influence on John Ruskin. This 1857 painting is by Robert Scott Tait.*

Octavia probably felt her skills were best utilised as campaigner rather than caretaker, so chose not to hold office in the National Trust, though she was a member of the committee. She was content to let Hunter, as Chairman, and Rawnsley, as Secretary, oversee the operations of the Trust while she continued her multifaceted campaigns for the betterment of society as Treasurer of her beloved Kyrle Society.

It is noteworthy that some two-thirds of the donors listed in Octavia's annual series of *Letters to My Fellow Workers* were women. Indeed, the National Trust grew out of an unheralded women's movement.

Octavia's Influence

'We have been very happy in securing a great many fresh workers, who have come in most heartily to join in what we are doing.'

Octavia Hill, *Letter to My Fellow Workers*

By the time the National Trust was formed, Octavia's fellow workers were already established in many other towns and cities, including Manchester, Leeds, Liverpool and Bristol. They also came from Holland, Germany, Sweden, Ireland, Italy – and America, where the Octavia Hill Association of Philadelphia still flourishes. Her proven methods of lean, friendly management became well known as applicable in urban conditions anywhere.

One of Octavia's oldest friends, Emma Cons, had worked in Lambeth for many years. As part of her housing operations she purchased the Royal Victoria Coffee and Music Hall (now the Old Vic Theatre), staging theatrical productions in a 'cheap and decent place of amusement on strict temperance lines'. Emma won a place on the London School Board and helped develop the nearby Morley College for Working Men and Women, which started out backstage in the theatre. She also managed the nearby Surrey Buildings using Octavia's methods.

From the late 1890s, the official system of clearance and rebuilding by the new London Council and other London boroughs began to rival Octavia's model management approach. She remained sceptical of those who placed all their hopes in central and local authority attempts to solve society's problems. For her, the redemption of society would come not through administrative, bureaucratic or utopian visions, but through the quiet assumption of mutual responsibilities towards each other by all individuals.

◄ The Old Vic, London, c.1926. It was once described by Charles Kingsley as 'a licensed pit of darkness, a trap of temptation, profligacy and ruin'. When acquired by Emma Cons, she dropped the word 'theatre' from the title because of its 'impure associations'.

◄ Samuel and Henrietta Barnett who founded Toynbee Hall in 1884. Later residents included Clement Attlee, who served as Britain's Prime Minister from 1945 to 1951.

Settlements

Octavia had introduced one of her co-workers, Samuel Barnett, to Henrietta Rowland, who became his wife, and 'dispatched them to the East End where the need was greatest'. There they established Toynbee Hall, the first University Settlement, named after historian Arnold Toynbee. Both Toynbee Hall and Octavia's own Women's University Settlement were imitated worldwide as community service and social study centres. Such settlements were devised as 'a house among the poor where residents may make friends with the poor'. It was believed that if men and women from universities lived for some time among the poor, they could 'do a little to remove the inequalities of life'.

Octavia the Rebel

'Gentlemen think if they put a water-closet to every room they have made a home of it.'
Octavia Hill

Octavia's Red Cross site had been started the year before the new London County Council was formed. The LCC began to tackle the housing problem with well-intentioned zeal. Octavia became increasingly out of step with mainstream reformist opinion on the housing question; although respectful of their efforts, she had always signalled her reservations about the work of commercial and philanthropic companies. They built their blocks on slum clearance sites and catered for higher-status artisans rather than the poor people who originally lived there. 'A third-rate cottage with a small garden, or even a back-yard, is better for a working man than that best tenement that the London County Council can build ... because when the tenant can command his own front door and staircase, he can preserve the unity of his family,' she said.

Years earlier John Ruskin had observed that Octavia's work, though admirable, was only ameliorative. Only state action could be radically curative. Octavia, however, thought it would create two worlds: those who lived in ghettos of municipal houses and those who did not. Her aim was to bridge the class divide, not accentuate it. She wanted to 'promote the happy, natural intercourse of neighbours ... members of households, as we are ourselves, instead of contemplating them as a different class'. Her aim was a blended community where all citizens knew, or knew of, each other.

Votes for women

Octavia was outspoken in her opposition to the 'votes for women' movement. At the root of Octavia's thinking was her mentor Frederick Denison Maurice, whose scepticism of the political process as a mechanism for solving the problems of society had so influenced her. It was not that Octavia undervalued women, but that she saw the limitations of politics. For her, women had – and should continue to have – a role in society that was distinct from that of men. Women were better able to engage at a human level with problems and would dissipate their natural skills in the talking shop of Parliament. She knew that their role behind the scenes of the public arena had been quietly effective.

▼ *Octavia Hill (front row, third from right) and the Poor Law Commission Committee, 1907. As a Commissioner she was one of only a few women to be involved with the male-dominated Committee.*

Preserving the Countryside

*'Kent and Surrey are the natural playground and resting place for those,
rich and poor, whose home is in our smoky, noisy London.'*

Octavia Hill

Always prone to overwork, Octavia Hill found rest and relaxation at Crockham Hill, a village near Edenbridge in Kent, where in 1884 she and Harriot Yorke built Larksfield, a cottage which afforded magnificent views across the Kentish Weald. Her home became a base for campaigns to save open spaces and footpaths, both local and national.

All the three founders of the National Trust – Hill, Hunter and Rawnsley – were active in the defence of footpaths and public rights of way and, in 1888, Octavia Hill helped to persuade the Commons Preservation Society to add footpaths to its remit. She said they were 'one of the great common inheritances to which English citizens are born. Once lost, these paths can never be regained. Let us before it is too late unite to preserve them'. The area around her home is criss-crossed by the footpaths that were saved by her and her associates. In 1930, Sir Lawrence Chubb (1873–1948), Secretary of the National Trust, wrote: 'When the time comes for the historian to apportion the credit to those who have helped to save the commons and footpaths of England for the enjoyment of the whole community, I have no doubt that he will attribute much of the success to the influence and self-sacrificing work of Octavia Hill.'

> ### Hills and headlands
>
> More than 30 years earlier, during her 1875 battle to save Swiss Cottage Fields, Octavia had referred to a 'green belt' – the first recorded use of the term. Typically, in her last years she began to make her vision a reality. Mariners Hill, Toys Hill and Ide Hill in Kent, all commanding magnificent views, were given to the National Trust. On Mariners Hill, there is a stone plinth that reads: 'The preservation of Mariners Hill as an open space property was due to the efforts of Octavia Hill.' At Toys Hill, Octavia bought and presented to the National Trust one of its first properties, where a terrace – with a well sunk to bring water to the village – commands a view across the Weald. Subsequent gifts have added substantially to the National Trust estate in the area.

Pioneer to the End

'When I am gone, I hope my friends will not try to carry out any special system, or to follow blindly in the track which I have trodden.'
Octavia Hill, speaking on her 60th birthday

In 1906, the Ecclesiastical Commissioners began to lay out the 22-acre (9-ha) Walworth Estate near the Elephant and Castle area of London. The Walworth Estate was the largest development of its kind, and remarkable in that Octavia Hill persuaded the Ecclesiastical Commissioners to allow her and her colleagues to both design and manage it. At a time when much attention was given to the developments of Hampstead Garden Suburb and Letchworth Garden City, in Hertfordshire, Octavia remained committed to improving the inner city.

The area, with its hundreds of one-storey cottages, had been compared to 'some out-of-the-way country district: the quacking of ducks and crowing of cocks were as frequently heard as the barrel organ ... we were sometimes greeted at the door when calling for the rent by the coster's donkey'. The design for the new estate featured a mix of cottages, cottage flats and three-storey tenement houses, recreational open space and a community hall. It was, in fact, the Red Cross development writ large. With its 790 houses, it answered critics who claimed that Octavia's small-scale development models could not achieve the urban density necessary to house the population of London. Notably, the clearance and redevelopment process ensured that the same people who had lived there were rehoused on the site. Significantly, too, with echoes of the Wisbech days, the local shop was a co-operative store.

For three years, although already suffering from breast cancer, Octavia Hill travelled the country as a Commissioner charged with reviewing the Poor Laws which had been in place since the 1830s. At this time she also piloted a scheme for lady district visitors independent of her housing work in Southwark. In one of her social work histories, Katherine A. Kendall, President of the International Association of Schools of Social Work, wrote: 'It all began with Octavia Hill.'

Octavia died, aged 73, on 13 August 1912 at her London home, 190 Marylebone Road. Marylebone Road itself still has trees planted by the Kyrle Society and its allies. She is buried beneath a yew tree in the churchyard at Crockham Hill in Kent, not far from Larksfield.

▼ *Octavia Hill is buried with her sister Miranda and companion Harriot Yorke in Crockham Hill churchyard.*

◄ *The view from Toys Hill to Ide Hill.*

After Octavia

'Miss Hill's work has lost a little of its special interest. It had proved its case. It had converted the world.'
Henry Scott Holland (1847–1918), Canon of Christ Church, Oxford

Following Octavia's death, her work continued, not only in England but around the world. During the First World War the Ministry of Munitions and other departments employed Octavia Hill workers. The Association of Women Housing Managers, started in 1916, carried on her pioneering work, deploying her workers around the country and abroad in, for example, South Africa and Hong Kong; it evolved as a formal training organisation, eventually amalgamating with what is now the Chartered Institute of Housing. Octavia Hill's managers were hired to oversee the developments of new towns, such as Welwyn Garden

Landscape memorials

When John Ruskin died in 1900, Octavia opposed the proposed monument to him in Westminster Abbey, saying that a preserved plot of countryside would be a better memorial. The National Trust had always been influenced by the Report of the Massachusetts Trustees for Public Reservations which asked: 'Is not a religiously guarded landscape a finer monument than any ordinary work in marble or stained glass?' Ruskin was subsequently buried in Coniston, in the Lake District. Octavia's memorial was the National Trust's 600-feet (182-m) high Hydon's Ball in Surrey; the hilltop was laid out by landscape gardener Gertrude Jekyll.

▼ *Detail from the Centenary Mural in Octavia Hill's Birthplace House showing personalities connected with the National Trust from 1895–1995, including Professor Chorley, Viscount Esher, the Marquess of Zetland, the Duke of Grafton, Dame Jennifer Jenkins and Harriot Yorke.*

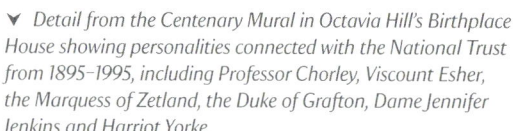

▲ *The badge of the National Trust of Australia, established in 1945.*

◀ The Octavia Hill Society marked its 20th anniversary in 2011 with the naming of the Octavia Hill geranium.

City in Hertfordshire, founded in 1920. However, some of her successors did not agree with her anti-municipal stand and were employed by Local Authorities.

In the first Octavia Hill memorial lecture in 1994, Richard (now Lord) Best – a leader of British social housing and one of the first men to work with these women managers – said: 'An abiding impression of the people I have known who walked in Octavia's footsteps is their down-to-earth, no-nonsense approach. These women were not theorists or dreamers even though strong moral principles underpinned their work.'

▶ Octavia Hill's secretary, Maud Jeffery (pictured here with students), was trained by her employer and later was in charge of the Crown Estate near Regent's Park in London.

The National Trust – remembering Octavia

As part of the celebrations for its centenary in 1995, the National Trust asked Harkness Roses to develop a new rose called 'Octavia Hill'; this delicate pink bloom can be seen in the garden at Chartwell, Winston Churchill's former home in Kent, now a National Trust property. Philip Harkness also donated the 'Our Place' rose as an emblem for the Octavia Hill Society's Hundred Schools Centenary Project. Additionally, she is remembered in Kent by Octavia Hill Basecamp (one of the 40 National Trust volunteer bases), renamed in her honour in the Trust's centenary year.

◀ The Octavia Hill rose.

Octavia Today
The Living Legacy

One of the aims of the Octavia Hill Society, founded in 1992, was to establish a museum in her memory in the Birthplace House. In 1994, with the help of Octavia's descendants in the Ouvry and Hill families and a public appeal chaired by Lady Chorley (whose husband and father-in-law were both past chairmen of the National Trust), the Octavia Hill Birthplace Museum Trust purchased part of the Wisbech house. Following its expansion as a museum, aided by HLF and EEDA grants, visitors can now learn the remarkable story of her life and work in a sequence of display rooms and in the River of Life garden based on Ruskin's *The King of the Golden River* fairy tale.

Octavia Hill's Birthplace House
7 South Brink
Wisbech
Cambridgeshire PE13 1JB
Tel: 01945 476358
Email: info@octaviahill.org
Website: http://octaviahill.org/birthplace-house.html

Listed here are some of the other organisations and charities with links to the world of Octavia Hill:

National Trust: www.nationaltrust.org.uk
Angles Theatre, Wisbech: http://home.btconnect.com/ANGLES-THEATRE
Army Cadets: www.armycadets.com
Bankside Open Spaces Trust: www.bost.org.uk
Blackfriars Settlement (previously Women's University Settlement): www.blackfriars-settlement.org.uk
Brantwood (former home of John Ruskin): www.brantwood.org.uk
British Association of Occupational Therapists: www.cot.co.uk
Family Action: www.family-action.org.uk
Hong Kong Housing Association: www.hkhs.com
Joseph Rowntree Foundation: www.jrf.org.uk
Metropolitan Public Gardens Association: www.mpga.org.uk
New Lanark World Heritage Site: www.newlanark.org
Open Spaces Society: www.oss.org.uk
Octavia Hill Association, Philadelphia: www.octaviahill.com
Octavia Hill Society: http://octaviahill.org/the-octavia-hill-society.html
Octavia Housing: www.octaviahousing.org.uk
The Society for the Protection of Ancient Buildings: www.spab.org.uk
Toynbee Hall: www.toynbeehall.org.uk
Working Men's College (for women and men): www.wmcollege.ac.uk

MAKING DEMOCRACY WORK FOR PRO-POOR DEVELOPMENT

Report of the
Commonwealth Expert Group on
Development and Democracy

*Manmohan Singh
Jocelyne Bourgon
Robert Champion de Crespigny AC
Richard Jolly
Martin Khor
Akinjide Osuntokun
Salim Ahmed Salim
Tuiloma Neroni Slade
Dwight Venner
Ngaire Woods*

The Expert Group is indebted to Dr S.K. Rao for his background paper which greatly assisted their discussion.

COMMONWEALTH SECRETARIAT

© The Commonwealth Secretariat, October 2003

All rights reserved.

The views expressed in this document do not necessarily reflect the official position or policy of the Commonwealth Secretariat or any other agency or government identified.

Layout design: Tina Johnson
Cover design: Tattersall, Hammarling and Silk
Printed in Britain by: Formara Ltd.
Published by: The Commonwealth Secretariat

Copies of this publication may be ordered directly from:
The Publications Manager
Communications and Public Affairs Division
Commonwealth Secretariat
Marlborough House
Pall Mall, London SW1Y 5HX
United Kingdom
Tel: +44 (0) 20 7747 6342
Fax: +44 (0) 20 7839 9081
E-mail: r.jones-parry@commonwealth.int

ISBN: 0-85092-781-1

Price: £10.99

This report was prepared by Roman Krznaric in co-operation with the Commonwealth Secretariat, based on meetings of the Commonwealth Expert Group on Development and Democracy. The meetings took place on 11-12 November 2002, 1-2 May 2003 and 24-25 July 2003 at the Commonwealth Secretariat, Marlborough House, London.

Contents

Foreword by the Commonwealth Secretary-General		iii
Letter of Presentation		v
Executive Summary		vii

1	Introduction		1
	1.1	The mandate	1
	1.2	Overview	1

2	A New Approach to Development and Democracy		5
	2.1	What is pro-poor development?	6
	2.2	What is democracy?	8
	2.3	Making democracy work for pro-poor development	12
	2.4	The key partnership: states, markets, civil society and the international community	15

3	Poverty in the Commonwealth		19

4	National Measures to Support Development and Democracy		25
	4.1	State administration	25
	4.2	Pro-poor economic and social policies	28
	4.3	Recommended actions at the national level	35

5	International Measures to Promote Development and Democracy		41
	5.1	The global economy	41
	5.2	International institutions	56
	5.3	Peace and security	59
	5.4	Recommended actions at the international level	64

6	Conclusion		69

References		75

Appendix A:	Progress towards the Millennium Development Goals in Commonwealth Countries	81
Appendix B:	Millennium Development Goals, Targets and Indicators	96
Appendix C:	Data on Development and Democracy in the Commonwealth	99
Appendix D:	Members of the Commonwealth Expert Group on Development and Democracy	105

Foreword

The Commonwealth has spelt out its commitment to development and to its fundamental political values in various declarations. There is already an understanding of how development and poverty alleviation can be promoted through concerted action at the national and international levels. This has been best articulated in the Monterrey Consensus. In addition, there is now considerable knowledge about how we can promote democratic processes and institutions, the rule of law, the independence of the judiciary, just and honest government and fundamental rights. Despite the knowledge and understanding that we have at our disposal, however, the record in terms of promoting development and democracy remains mixed.

It is now widely recognised that development is about much more than growth of GDP. Equally, everyone appreciates that democracy is more than simply a matter of universal suffrage and the holding of regular multiparty elections, essential though these are. So we need to understand exactly what is meant by development and democracy today, in the twenty-first century. Furthermore, while development and democracy are goals in their own right, they must also be mutually reinforcing. A key challenge is to understand how best to make this a reality.

These are crucial issues that must be addressed if the mixed record of promoting development and democracy within the Commonwealth, and the wider world, is to be improved.

Commonwealth Heads of Government called on me to constitute a high level Expert Group to recommend ways in which democracies might best be supported in combating poverty. I was fortunate in being able to secure the services of a highly distinguished group of people under the very experienced Chairmanship of Dr Manmohan Singh, the former Finance Minister of India. All the members served on the Group in their individual capacities. Representatives of the International Monetary Fund (IMF) and World Bank also participated in the work of the Group.

I am commending this Report for the consideration of the Commonwealth Heads of Government at their meeting in Abuja (5-8 December 2003). I hope it will enable the Commonwealth to provide leadership in mobilising partnerships to meet the twin challenges of promoting development and democracy. Improved performance on both fronts is essential to secure global peace and prosperity.

Don McKinnon, *Commonwealth Secretary-General*

Letter of Presentation

Marlborough House
London

30 September 2003

HE Donald C McKinnon
Commonwealth Secretary-General
Marlborough House
London SW1Y 5HX

Dear Secretary-General,

In accordance with the wishes of Commonwealth Heads of Government at their meeting in Coolum, Australia, in March 2002, you appointed us to recommend ways in which we could carry forward the Fancourt Commonwealth Declaration of 1999, focusing on how democracies might best be supported in combating poverty. We now present our Report, which we have signed in our personal capacities and not as representatives of the governments, organisations or countries to which we belong.

The Expert Group believes that the Commonwealth can make more of its comparative advantage with respect to other regional and global bodies to confront the crisis of global poverty and the failure of many developing countries to consolidate and deepen democracy. Commonwealth countries and institutions are in a strong position to support both development and democracy in member states. Commonwealth membership in all key world forums also enables it to be a powerful advocate for change at the international level. The Group suggests that membership carries with it the obligation for member countries to make every effort to advance Commonwealth principles in all other forums to which they belong. The Recommendations in this Report contain suggestions for Commonwealth Heads of Government about how these objectives can be advanced.

In our discussions we have benefited from the participation of Mr Masood Ahmed (IMF) and Mr Alan Gelb (World Bank). We are grateful for their contributions.

We are also grateful to you for the confidence you showed in asking us to undertake this task, and to your staff for the support they have given us.

Yours sincerely,

Manmohan Singh

Jocelyne Bourgon

Robert Champion de Crespigny AC

Richard Jolly

Martin Khor

Akinjide Osuntokun

Salim Ahmed Salim

Tuiloma Neroni Slade

Dwight Venner

Ngaire Woods

Executive Summary

Making Democracy Work for Pro-poor Development

1. What can be done to confront the crisis of global poverty and the failure of many developing countries to consolidate and deepen democracy? This Report, which contains the findings of the Commonwealth Expert Group on Development and Democracy, identifies priorities for action by Commonwealth Heads of Government to help tackle these problems. A new generation of national and international public policies is urgently required. The Report emphasises the central role of states, markets and civil society, and focuses on development policies that in themselves uphold and promote democratic values.

2. In short, this Report is about making democracy work for pro-poor development. The Commonwealth's commitment to development and democracy was expressed in the Harare Commonwealth Declaration of 1991 and the Fancourt Commonwealth Declaration of 1999. The Commonwealth Expert Group on Development and Democracy was established by the Commonwealth Secretary-General in pursuance of the following mandate given by Commonwealth Heads of Government at their meeting in Coolum, Australia, in March 2002:

> "Recognising the links between democracy and good governance on the one hand, and poverty, development and conflict on the other, we call on the Commonwealth Secretary-General to constitute a high-level expert group to recommend ways in which we could carry forward the Fancourt Declaration. This group should focus on how democracies might best be supported in combating poverty, and should report to the next CHOGM."

3. The Expert Group, comprising ten experts from a range of disciplines and professional backgrounds related to international development and good governance, met three times in 2002 and 2003 to prepare its Report.

Progress towards Democracy and Development

4. As the Commonwealth enters the twenty-first century, democracy and development are under threat. Terrorism, military intervention and over 50 major internal armed conflicts in the past decade have exacted a high cost for both democracy and for pro-poor development. HIV/AIDS is devastating whole communities, particularly in sub-Saharan Africa, overstretching the capabilities and resources of governments and highlighting the need for more immediate and more effective multilateral action.

5. Given the conflicts and tensions in the world today, and the seriousness of many of the divides between countries, religions and ethnic groups, reducing poverty and improving governance are more important than ever. They are directly needed for peace and stability and are essential steps for the world to move towards greater international equality and justice.

6. Despite the global challenges there remains cause for hope. The Millennium Development Goals (MDGs) have mobilised governments, international institutions and civil society to tackle poverty in new ways and with unprecedented commitment. Moreover, democratic institutions and human rights have become accepted political ambitions for peoples all over the world.

Development and Democracy in the Commonwealth

7. How is the Commonwealth performing in this uncertain context? The statistics on development are both clear and overwhelming. Overall the performance is extremely disturbing and calls for collective remedial action.

- One third of the Commonwealth's two billion people live on less than one dollar a day and nearly two thirds on under two dollars a day.

- 60 per cent of global HIV cases are in the Commonwealth, and four of the nine most affected countries are Commonwealth members. Nearly 60 per cent of Commonwealth citizens lack access to essential drugs and adequate sanitation facilities.

- Around half of the world's 115 million children without access to primary school live in the Commonwealth.

- Women constitute around 70 per cent of those living in poverty in the Commonwealth.

- Young people constitute over 50 per cent of the Commonwealth population. A large percentage of them are adversely affected by unemployment, poverty, HIV/AIDS and illiteracy.

- Of the 31 countries classified by UNDP's *Human Development Report 2003* as 'top priority' due to their overall slow or reversing progress towards the MDGs, nine are from the Commonwealth: Cameroon, Kenya, Lesotho, Mozambique, Nigeria, Sierra Leone, United Republic of Tanzania, Zambia and Zimbabwe. The situation may be even more serious given that there are insufficient data available to classify 13 Commonwealth states on their progress towards the MDGs.

8. There are, however, several Commonwealth countries that have made significant progress towards the MDGs. For instance, 11 countries in the Commonwealth have made fast progress towards the goal of halving the number of people who suffer from hunger by 2015 (Section 3).

9. With respect to democracy, the global political landscape has changed dramatically in recent decades. Twenty-five years ago there were some 35 democracies in the world, most of them in the wealthy industrialised nations. Today there are around 130. Many of these new democracies are in the Commonwealth, but we believe democratic processes and institutions could be strengthened in a number of them with a unified effort. Yet several Commonwealth countries have not established basic democratic procedures such as free and fair multiparty elections, or managed to respect, protect and fulfil the full range of human rights. Women constitute on average only 13.4 per cent of parliamentarians in the Commonwealth as a whole, far below the 30 per cent target set by Commonwealth Heads of Government. Despite the long history of democratic governance in some Commonwealth countries, in others there is an urgent need to encourage democratic reforms.

The Commonwealth Contribution

10. The Commonwealth has already made important contributions to supporting both democracy and development. It has been involved in conflict resolution and peace-building in the Pacific, Africa and the Caribbean, including through the use of the Secretary-General's good offices. The Commonwealth Ministerial Action Group exercises peer pressure on member countries violating democratic principles. The Commonwealth plays a vital role in election observation in addition to providing technical assistance to strengthen the institutions required for democratic governance and the development of pro-poor national economic and social policy.

11. The Expert Group believes, however, that the Commonwealth must make more of its comparative advantage with respect to other regional and global bodies. The Commonwealth is a unique microcosm of global social and ethnic diversity, and of North and South. Commonwealth countries and institutions are in a strong position to help deepen democracy and support development in member states. The Recommendations in this Report contain suggestions for Commonwealth Heads of Government about how this can be done.

The Key Partnership: States, Markets, Civil Society and the International Community

12. This Report argues that the state, the market, civil society and the international community each has a vital role to play in delivering development and democracy.

That said, the foundations of democratic development lie in democratic and accountable institutions of government.

States

13. A strong, effective, accountable state is the first pillar of democracy and development. Neither can be imported. International institutions alone cannot and should not take responsibility for eradicating poverty, authoritarianism and conflict. National governments should take the initiative by ensuring that their own core institutions of democracy are fully accountable, and by adopting pro-poor development strategies and promoting democratic reforms and human rights at all levels – in local government, at the national level, and in the international organisations in which they participate.

14. The foundations of a democratic state are worth recalling:

- a freely and fairly elected parliament that is broadly representative of the people of the country;
- an executive (government) that is answerable to parliament;
- an independent judiciary;
- a police force that responds to the law for its operations and the government for its administration; and
- armed forces that are answerable to government and parliament.

15. For democracy to survive and function properly each of these institutions must be held to account. This requires:

- an independent electoral commission;
- an independent human rights commission;
- a freedom of information commission; and
- an ombudsman.

16. Furthermore, at the heart of democracy and development lie the resources of a nation. It is imperative that parliament is the only channel through which the executive is funded and that the public accounts system be transparent and straightforward, clearly reflecting where money is coming from and where it is going to.

17. The financial affairs of any democratic government should be monitored by parliament through a public accounts committee, and by an auditor-general answerable to parliament (Section 4.1).

Markets

18. Markets have an essential place in the pursuit of development and democracy. Economic growth fuelled by market competition can contribute to many, if not all, aspects of poverty reduction. Domestic and cross-border private investment provides the majority of resources that currently finance development. The private sector can take up responsibilities as a partner in the quest for pro-poor development and democracy. Codes of corporate governance and practices that demonstrate a respect for democratic institutions and culture, that promote human rights (particularly labour rights), that prohibit corruption and that are properly enforced and monitored by companies are all part of that responsibility (Section 5.1).

Civil society

19. Civil society is the third pillar of pro-poor development and democratisation. Building the capacity of citizens' organisations and a free and well-informed media are critical for promoting citizen participation, holding government to account and empowering poor communities. Poor people and poor communities, for example, are in the best position to understand and articulate their own needs, and their voices should be heard directly within government. But often they are not and here political rights and opportunities can be bolstered through community action. The media plays an important role both in giving voice to citizens and in holding government and the private sector to account on their behalf. The responsibility of civil society is to ensure that their own practices respect democratic values such as tolerance and accountability, and that their actions positively promote pro-poor development and the strengthening of democratic culture (Section 2.2). Equally, the media have a responsibility to set high professional standards and to encourage and reward responsible journalism.

The international community

20. Beyond the state, the market and civil society, there is a need for action in the international community. The wealthier industrialised countries must not impede development through their own protectionist measures, including subsidies and restrictions on market access in agriculture and textiles. They must promote and work within a rules-based and transparent multilateral trading system that is more responsive to the needs of poor countries. Having committed themselves to the MDGs and to the New Partnership for Africa's Development (NEPAD), the industrialised countries must now implement their pledges, providing resources in ways that promote democracy and development. Specifically, this means providing debt relief that releases adequate resources for governments to pursue development programmes, particularly in the areas of health and education, and increasing untied official aid

and direct budgetary support to the levels needed to attain the MDGs. Where international economic organisations such as the International Monetary Fund (IMF), the World Bank and the World Trade Organisation (WTO) set down conditionality or constraints on policy, it must be in the pursuit of pro-poor development, and must work in ways that do not erode democratic institutions and human rights at the national and sub-national levels (Section 5.2). Finally, in respect of war and armed conflict, when domestic efforts have been made and have failed, the international community must take action to reduce conflict and insecurity (Section 5.3).

Responsibility and partnership

21. This Report is a call for responsibility, partnership and concrete actions – from governments, from the private sector, from civil society and from the international community. Without responsibility on all these levels, development and democracy will remain rhetoric rather than become reality. While development and democracy are goals in their own right, they can and should be mutually reinforcing. To promote peace and prosperity, Commonwealth Heads of Government must commit to a new, deeper approach to development and democracy.

A New Approach to Development and Democracy

22. The Expert Group approaches the problems of development and democracy that exist in the Commonwealth and elsewhere on the basis of two guiding priorities:

1. Pro-poor development

23. Rather than focusing on development in general, this Report concentrates specifically on *pro-poor development* (Section 2.1). This emphasises two particular aspects of human development and policy. First, it is a vision of development that recognises that people need the 'capabilities' to do and be the things that they have reason to value, such as being adequately nourished, having equitable access to justice and participating in decisions that affect their lives. Second, it recognises that development policies aimed at the general populace may have a more limited positive impact on particularly disadvantaged groups. Policies that promote economic growth and a sound macroeconomic framework cannot always be relied upon to improve the lives of those in poor communities. Disadvantaged groups need to be identified (for example, in terms of gender, ethnicity, religion, age or occupation) and policies need to be specifically designed for improving the lives of the poor.

2. *Democracy underpinned by accountable institutions and a democratic culture*

24. The Expert Group believes that democracy must be based on representative

institutions that are held fully to account and operate to monitor and restrain any possible abuse of public power or the public purse. Free, fair and independently monitored multiparty elections are one element of this. Equally important are the institutions that check and oversee the power and financial management of the executive or government, including the judiciary, parliament, ombudsman, and independent commissions created by government to fulfil this role. Finally, the police forces in democracies must respond to the law for their operations and the government for their administration, while the armed forces must be responsible for the defence of the country. Both should be answerable to the law and to the parliament, not to individuals or to political parties.

25. Beyond these core institutions, democracy requires the preservation and reinforcement of a democratic culture. This requires:

- *Respect for human rights* including political and civil rights such as freedom of speech and information and equality before the law; social and economic rights such as the right to an adequate standard of living in terms of food, clothing and housing, and the right to organise and collectively bargain; gender rights that prevent discrimination against women, such as the rights to personal security and redress against violence, to reproductive health and to equal pay for equal work; and group rights to protect those, such as indigenous peoples, who may suffer due to their religion, ethnicity or caste.

- *Representation and participation in the political process* by a wide variety of social groups in political institutions, especially disadvantaged groups such as women and minorities. This can be enhanced by strengthening local democracy.

- *Civic associations and a free media* that encourage citizens to hold their government to account, that promote the representation of disadvantaged groups and that enhance tolerance and strengthen the cohesion of diverse and multicultural societies.

26. The Expert Group's perspective on democracy firmly emphasises the importance of a country's practice, not merely its nominal commitments. It considers democracy to be meaningful in people's lives when it is put into effect rather than simply enshrined as constitutional or legal principles.

Recommendations

27. In a global context that provides both challenges and opportunities, the Expert Group has made a number of recommendations on the national and international

levels to promote development and democracy. These are specified in Sections 4.3 and 5.4. The Group wishes to highlight its most significant recommendations that it hopes will be considered priorities for action by Commonwealth Heads of Government and Commonwealth institutions.

1. Committing to core democratic institutions

28. For national measures to be effective in making development and democracy mutually reinforcing, Commonwealth governments should commit to ensuring that the following core institutions exist in their own countries and are fully held to account.

- A freely and fairly elected **parliament** that is broadly representative of the people of the country and whose election is overseen by an independent electoral commission.

- An **executive** (government) that is answerable to – and funded solely through – the parliament.

- An independent **judiciary** (which means that judges must be financially secure during the period of their appointment and in retirement).

- A transparent and straightforward **public accounts system** (which clearly reflects where money is coming from and where it is going to) and a **public accounts committee**, responsible for monitoring public expenditure.

- An **auditor-general** answerable to parliament (i.e. the public accounts committee) ensuring, *inter alia*, the financial accountability of the executive.

- An independent **human rights commission** that protects citizens from discrimination and human rights abuses and ensures that the government treats all citizens equally.

- A **freedom of information commission** that enables the public to gain access to information about executive decisions and allows individuals to access information held about them by the police and public bodies.

- An **ombudsman**.

- A **police force** that responds to the law for its operations and the government for its administration.

- **Armed forces** that are answerable to government and parliament, not to political parties, and are responsible for the defence of the country.

29. The Group requests the Commonwealth Secretary-General to work with member governments to build and strengthen such an institutional framework, where necessary.

2. Protecting a strong democratic culture

30. At every level of government in the Commonwealth, democracy should be buttressed by a strong democratic culture that ensures that all citizens enjoy the full range of human rights. Freedom of information, freedom of assembly and freedom of the press and media are crucial. At the same time, the Commonwealth could and should be a positive force for celebrating cultural diversity and resisting the advance of fundamentalism and intolerance in every member country. Given the Commonwealth's experience of handling diversity, the Commonwealth Secretariat should seek to convey the positive aspects of cultural diversity – particularly in contexts where it has been negatively exploited to a divisive end – and demonstrate best practice.

31. The Group believes that local democracy, particularly the strengthening of elected local government and wide citizens' participation, including women and youth, is an important way to promote democratic values and deepen the democratic process.

3. Tackling corruption

32. At the national level throughout the Commonwealth, corruption and the looting of public funds should be tackled (as highlighted in the Report of the Commonwealth Expert Group on Good Governance and the Elimination of Corruption). Within national systems, Commonwealth governments can set core standards in respect of political party financing and codes of ethics and transparency regarding the interests of parliamentarians. At the international level, Commonwealth governments can promote transparency in the contracts between governments and corporations in extractive industries (as is advocated in the present Extractive Industries Transparency Initiative being promulgated by the UK Department for International Development). Finally, all Commonwealth governments need to actively aid fellow Commonwealth countries in the repatriation of illegally acquired public funds and assets that have been transferred abroad, including through the establishment of appropriate legal frameworks and through exploring the possibility of an international convention. The Expert Group believes that a Commonwealth Technical Working Group to examine the issues involved would help advance effective action in this area.

4. *Ensuring democratic accountability of government revenue and expenditure*

33. At the heart of democratic pro-poor development lies the process of government revenue and expenditure. The Expert Group emphasises that a sound and accountable system for drawing up budgets, implementing them and monitoring their impact is a key instrument for promoting pro-poor development and democracy and for building stable, cohesive societies. Throughout the Commonwealth this requires member governments to commit to creating budgetary processes that involve (particularly disadvantaged) citizens in consultation and participation on key issues. Equally important is to develop procedures for evaluating the impact of budgets on disadvantaged groups such as poor communities, women, children and youth. In addition, the public needs to understand the budget in order to hold the government to account. The Commonwealth Secretariat should develop a template to facilitate this.

34. A necessary complement to improvements in public expenditure management systems is for Commonwealth member governments to commit to introducing tax reforms, particularly improvements in tax administration, that generate more resources for pro-poor development.

5. *Promoting free and fair trade*

35. The existing multilateral trading system needs to be developed to support both pro-poor development and democracy more positively. The breakdown of negotiations at Cancun highlights the challenge powerful countries face in demonstrating their commitment to inclusive globalisation, attainment of the MDGs and global peace and security. Commonwealth governments could play a vital role in ensuring that ongoing negotiations address the asymmetries of the international trade regime discussed in this Report, such as those related to agriculture (including subsidies and dumping), market access for non-agricultural products, implementation of the trade-related aspects of intellectual property rights (TRIPS) agreement (particularly affordable drugs), and special and differential treatment. At the same time, it is vital that poor and vulnerable economies in the Commonwealth are permitted to undertake liberalisation in ways and with phasing that minimise transition costs and do not impact harshly upon the poor within those countries.

36. The Group notes that the Commonwealth Secretariat could usefully expand its programmes to provide technical support to developing Commonwealth countries as a means of increasing their capacity to negotiate and implement their obligations within the WTO system in ways that are consistent with their development interests. In addition, where there is significant convergence on particular trade issues, the Commonwealth should bring the full weight of the association to bear on advancing the agenda.

6. Financing for development

37. Poor countries need urgent and substantive increases in the quantity and quality of financial resources if they are to achieve pro-poor development and the MDGs. The Group believes that such resources can be made available by the international community through a number of means and in particular:

(i) innovative mechanisms for increasing official development assistance (ODA) such as the UK proposal for an International Finance Facility that, if not taken up by all countries, could be adapted as a Commonwealth mechanism for raising development resources;

(ii) improving aid effectiveness through, *inter alia,* strengthened aid administration in beneficiary countries, reductions in tied aid and an increase in direct budgetary support, and implementation of the Rome Declaration on Harmonisation;

(iii) support for social safety nets to reduce the impact of poverty on the most vulnerable groups, e.g., women, children, disadvantaged ethnic groups and indigenous peoples;

(iv) more flexible approaches to debt relief that release adequate resources to support domestically formulated and internationally agreed development programmes, particularly in health and education;

(v) support for measures that enhance greater stability of flows of private investment to developing countries; and

(vi) international financing initiatives to assist developing countries (particularly the smallest and most vulnerable) in confronting exogenous shocks such as a sharp deterioration in their terms of trade that threaten to derail otherwise robust development programmes. This could take the form of strengthening IMF and World Bank facilities to enable them to provide more timely, more concessional and more adequate assistance in these circumstances.

38. In respect of all these initiatives and strategies, the Group emphasises that the Commonwealth has a great opportunity to give a lead to the international community to ensure that resources for development are allocated and targeted in accordance with the recipient country's own development programmes and frameworks. Failure in this regard will not only undermine the long-term prospects for

economic success but will also undermine the democratic processes outlined above.

7. *International institutions*

39. International institutions, including the IMF, the World Bank, the WTO and the United Nations and its specialised agencies are all playing important roles in facilitating development, reducing poverty and securing the peace. The Group's concern is to ensure that international organisations pursue these goals in ways that reinforce and strengthen democratic decision-making and democratic culture within countries. In this regard, Commonwealth governments are urged:

- to encourage deeper participation of poor communities and vulnerable groups in the poverty reduction strategy paper (PRSP) processes of the IMF and World Bank, and to monitor the extent to which other policies and programmes of the IMF, the World Bank and the WTO might be bypassing or otherwise inadvertently eroding democratic processes and institutions at the national and sub-national levels; and

- to ensure that international institutions (such as the IMF, the World Bank, the WTO and UN institutions such as the Security Council) are themselves models of good practice in respect of democratic accountability, participation and transparency.

40. The Commonwealth should take advantage of the reach its members have into these institutions to develop productive working relationships with them in order to advance the association's values and objectives.

8. *Peace and security*

41. Conflict and insecurity extinguish the prospects of both democracy and development. Furthermore they impact disproportionately on the poorest in any society. Yet international action in the cases of the poorest and most desperate states in conflict is almost always dilatory and inadequate where domestic efforts to contain conflict have been made and failed. In Africa many Commonwealth states are at risk. The Group is particularly concerned that where regional and sub-regional organisations are attempting to address conflict situations such as those in Burundi, Democratic Republic of the Congo and Liberia, the international community is often failing to provide the timely logistical and financial support without which the operations cannot succeed. On this issue Commonwealth Heads of Government can make a difference by actively helping to mobilise critical international support and resources to facilitate the work of sub-regional or regional peace initiatives that are duly authorised by the United Nations Security Council.

9. Monitoring of progress towards development and democracy

42. Reports such as this generally fail to improve the environment for which they are written if there is not a definite, measurable monitoring of progress that is regularly and clearly reported to stakeholders. The Expert Group stresses the value of developing a means of monitoring progress towards implementing the above recommendations. It therefore requests the Commonwealth Secretariat to develop an appropriate framework for providing progress reports to Commonwealth Heads of Government at their biennial summits.

Manmohan Singh

Jocelyne Bourgon

Robert Champion de Crespigny AC

Richard Jolly

Martin Khor

Akinjide Osuntokun

Salim Ahmed Salim

Tuiloma Neroni Slade

Dwight Venner

Ngaire Woods

1
Introduction

1.1 The Mandate

43. The Expert Group on Development and Democracy was established by the Commonwealth Secretary-General in pursuance of the following mandate given by Commonwealth Heads of Government at their meeting in Coolum, Australia, in March 2002:

44. "Recognising the links between democracy and good governance on the one hand, and poverty, development and conflict on the other, we call on the Commonwealth Secretary-General to constitute a high-level expert group to recommend ways in which we could carry forward the Fancourt Declaration. This group should focus on how democracies might best be supported in combating poverty, and should report to the next CHOGM."

45. In interpreting this mandate the Expert Group has drawn its inspiration from the shared values of development and democracy within Commonwealth member states as expressed in the Harare Commonwealth Declaration of 1991 and the Fancourt Commonwealth Declaration of 1999. The Harare Principles recognise the need to protect and promote the fundamental political values of the Commonwealth, including democratic processes and institutions, the rule of law and human rights. The Principles also demonstrate a commitment to sustainable development and the alleviation of poverty. The Fancourt Commonwealth Declaration on Globalisation and People-Centred Development calls for the forces of globalisation to be channelled towards the elimination of poverty and the empowerment of human beings to lead fulfilling lives. It emphasises the importance of democratic freedoms and good governance, and stresses that development processes should be participatory and give a voice to the poor and vulnerable. In both the Harare and Fancourt Declarations, development and democracy are considered not only as goals in their own rights, but as interdependent and mutually reinforcing.[1]

1.2 Overview

46. The central theme of this Report is that democracy and pro-poor development can and should be mutually reinforcing. It recognises that poor country democracies face particular challenges in the contemporary world that require urgent domestic and international action. The Report emphasises the central role of states, markets and civil society, and focuses on development policies that in themselves uphold and

promote democratic values. In short, this Report is about making democracy work for pro-poor development.

47. Development and democracy are complex processes, and it would be impossible for any report to provide a detailed analysis of every possible means of promoting them individually and together. The Expert Group has thus been selective in its attentions and focused on the interactions between development and democracy.

48. This Report is global in geographical scope and attempts to examine patterns of development and democracy worldwide. However, it pays special attention to the experiences of development and democracy throughout the Commonwealth, especially among the more vulnerable communities including small states.

49. The analysis begins in Section 2 by outlining a new approach to development and democracy and suggests that the crisis of global poverty and weaknesses of democratisation processes in many countries can be addressed by using democratically-oriented policies to tackle poverty. This approach, which must provide a role for each of the state, the market and civil society, has the potential to result in both pro-poor development and deeper democracy.

50. Section 3 examines the problem of poverty from a Commonwealth perspective.

51. In Section 4 the Report highlights major national obstacles to pro-poor development such as ineffective state administration, corruption, inadequate education and health systems, and environmental degradation. It argues that neither development nor democracy can be imported and that it is therefore essential for national governments, rather than international institutions, to take the lead in promoting pro-poor development and democracy (Section 4.1 and 4.2). The Expert Group provides specific policy recommendations, for instance to promote democratic accountability of government expenditure and revenue, that can be implemented at the national and sub-national level to ensure development and democracy (Section 4.3).

52. Section 5 focuses on the obstacles to pro-poor development and democracy that exist at the international level. First, the Report explores global economic problems concerning the international trade regime, private capital flows, debt and aid (Section 5.1). Second, it examines how international institutions could be reformed to promote development and democracy more effectively (Section 5.2). Third, it describes how conflict and insecurity have affected the pursuit of development and democracy (Section 5.3). The Group's policy recommendations at the international level are designed to encourage reforms in these three areas (Section 5.4).

53. Both Sections 4 and 5 highlight innovative and concrete policy responses from

particular organisations and governments around the globe, including some from the Commonwealth. These are case studies of 'exemplary good practice'. They are *not* blueprints for development that the Expert Group endorses as 'one size fits all' development solutions. Rather they provide practical ideas and inspiration for how it is possible to make democracy work for pro-poor development in the diverse contexts of the real world. By taking this approach the Expert Group hopes to refrain from timid platitudes and instead to open up vigorous debate around substantive options in complex policy arenas.

54. Section 6 contains the Expert Group's concluding remarks on development and democracy.

2
A New Approach to Development and Democracy

'I will give you a talisman...Recall the face of the poorest and weakest man whom you may have seen, and ask yourself if the step you contemplate is going to be of any use to him. Will he gain anything by it? Will it restore him to a control over his own life and destiny?...Then you will find your doubts and yourself melting away.'

Mahatma Gandhi[2]

55. As the Commonwealth enters the twenty-first century, progress towards both democracy and development is under threat. Terrorism and the spread of international organised crime have created new obstacles to the pursuit of these goals. During the past decade there have been over 50 major internal armed conflicts, many of which have spread beyond national borders to create regional instability. The mixed success of international military interventions has raised questions about the appropriate methods for promoting democracy and development. HIV/AIDS is devastating whole communities, particularly in sub-Saharan Africa. Small vulnerable states and least developed countries (LDCs) have been especially prone to these problems and the instability of the increasingly global economy.

56. Given the conflicts and tensions in the world today, and the seriousness of many of the divides between countries, religions and ethnic groups, reducing poverty and improving governance are more important than ever. They are directly needed for peace and stability and are essential steps for the world to move towards greater international equality and justice.

57. Despite the global challenges there remains cause for hope. The Millennium Development Goals (MDGs) have mobilised governments, international institutions and civil society to tackle poverty in new ways and with unprecedented commitment. Moreover, democratic institutions and human rights have become accepted political ambitions for peoples all over the world.

58. The Commonwealth has already made important contributions to supporting both democracy and development. It has been involved in conflict resolution and peace-building in the Pacific, Africa and the Caribbean, including through the use of the Secretary-General's good offices. The Commonwealth Ministerial Action Group exercises peer pressure on member countries violating democratic principles. Commonwealth institutions play vital roles in election observation, in addition to

providing technical assistance to strengthen the institutions required for democratic governance and the development of pro-poor national economic and social policy.

59. The Expert Group believes, however, that it is possible for the Commonwealth to make more of its comparative advantage with respect to other regional and global bodies. The Commonwealth is a unique microcosm of global social and ethnic diversity, and of North and South. Commonwealth countries and institutions are in a strong position to help deepen democracy and support development in member states. The Recommendations in this Report contain suggestions for Commonwealth Heads of Government about how this can be done.

60. The relationship between development and democracy has been a subject of great debate in recent decades. While the dynamics of the relationship remain contested, one certainty is that the meanings of the central terms have changed. Just as development can no longer be equated with simplistic objectives such as growth of GDP per capita, so too democracy cannot be reduced to the narrow post-World War II procedural definitions based on regular civilian elections and multiparty politics. As the world changes, the concepts used to understand that world must also transform. A first step in providing a new approach to development and democracy for the twenty-first century is to define both 'development' and 'democracy'.

2.1 What is Pro-Poor Development?

61. This Report emphasises *pro-poor development*. The Expert Group recognises and endorses four significant changes in development thinking in recent decades, which together inform the meaning of this term.

> - *Defining development as strengthening human capabilities*
> First, the principal aim of development no longer focuses on maximising marketable production of goods. The emphasis now is on expanding opportunities and strengthening human capacities to lead long, healthy, creative and fulfilling lives. Development is about enabling people to have the 'capabilities' to do and be the things that they have reason to value. Poverty can be defined as the deprivation of basic capabilities and development as the process of ensuring that the most basic capabilities are achieved by all. Although the list of desirable capabilities may differ from one society to another, current thinking is that basic capabilities include: being adequately nourished, avoiding preventable morbidity and premature mortality, being effectively sheltered, having a basic education, being able to ensure security of the person, having equitable access to justice, being able to appear in public without shame, being able to earn a livelihood and being able to take part in the life of a community.[3] Under this approach, issues of freedom and participation traditionally associated with democracy are also recognised to

be part of development itself. This stress on expanding human capabilities is central to the Fancourt Declaration.

- *Focusing on the poor*

Second, the scope of development policy has become broader, making 'pro-poor development' a vital additional analytical category that orients attention towards those people most in need. Recognising that 'development' is still used loosely in the policy world to refer to development strategies for poor countries, rather than particularly for poor people in those countries, the Expert Group believes that it is important to distinguish and promote 'pro-poor development'. Development policies aimed at the general population may have a more limited positive impact on particularly disadvantaged groups. Pro-poor development concerns those policies that are specifically designed to enhance the quality of the lives of the poor. This Report highlights ways of supporting pro-poor policies in many development realms, from social policy at the national level to international trade regimes. Pro-poor development is also concerned with ensuring that current and future generations are able to meet their basic capabilities through sustainable use of the planet's resources. These are themes at the heart of the Fancourt Declaration to which Commonwealth Heads of Government and civil society are committed.[4]

- *Identifying the poor*

The focus on 'pro-poor development' raises the issue of identifying the poor. This is a third area in which development thinking has changed. The poor used to be identified as a faceless mass or as a statistic. In contrast, current thinking is to specify the diverse population groups that suffer from basic deprivations and inadequate achievement of basic capabilities. These groups can be identified, for example, in terms of gender, ethnicity, religion, age or occupation. Since poverty has various dimensions some social groups may, for instance, be poor with respect to health, while others may be poor with respect to education. Particular effort must be made to identify those groups that are especially deprived (e.g., women) and vulnerable (e.g., those with HIV/AIDS). Such groups are entitled to special attention when resource constraints require setting priorities.[5]

- *Moving beyond the 'trickle down' view*

Fourth, the Expert Group recognises the empirical evidence that questions the association between economic growth and poverty reduction. Proponents of the 'trickle down' view of poverty reduction argue that the best way to help the poor is to make the economy grow.[6] Yet there is abundant evidence to suggest that growth is a necessary but not sufficient condition for poverty reduction. While in some contexts growth can create opportunities and reduce income inequality, in other contexts (such as in countries where the poor lack a 'voice' and powerful and wealthy elites are able to pursue their narrow self-interest) growth may have little effect on poverty and may, perversely, increase relative and even absolute poverty. These findings reinforce this Report's emphasis on pro-poor development strategies: Policies to increase economic growth must also enhance the lives of those in poor communities.[7] The pro-poor nature of growth is more important than its statistical rate.

2.2 What is Democracy?

62. The Expert Group believes that free and fair multiparty elections are central to any meaningful conception of democracy. The scope of democracy must, however, be widened beyond elections, so that democratic institutions and processes facilitate, protect and reinforce the full range of human rights.

63. Democracy requires realising in practice a range of values that are designed to give people a voice in their political governance and ensure liberty and equality. On the one hand are values relating to democratic *institutions* and on the other are values concerning *human rights*. This approach reflects the Harare Declaration, which places both democratic institutions and human rights at the core of the Commonwealth's fundamental political values. Realising the institutional values is necessary to ensure sovereignty of the people and an inclusive political process, while facilitating, protecting and reinforcing human rights upholds the rule of law and constitutional guarantees, and delivers the substance of democracy to citizens. The relevant values are as follows.

64. *Institutional values*

- *Accountability and transparency*

Governments should be accountable to citizens through free and fair elections that express the will of the people. Accountability also requires transparency of government through the elimination of corruption and operation of oversight mechanisms such as ombudsmen, auditors-general and parliamentary select committees. In addition, states should embody horizontal accountability, meaning that no one element of the state, such as the military or executive, can act unchecked by its other branches. Any relinquishment of sovereignty should go hand in hand with citizen consultation and the development of public accountability mechanisms. As will be discussed below, accountability and other democratic values can also be applied to non-state actors, such as international financial institutions, businesses and civil society.

- *Representation*

Elected officials must effectively represent their constituents, and institutions such as parliaments should take account of the interests of a wide variety of social groups. This is particularly important with respect to politically, economically and socially disadvantaged groups such as women and minorities, including indigenous peoples. Commonwealth Heads of Government set a target of 30 per cent of women in decision-making at their meeting in Edinburgh in 1997, but to date only three countries have achieved this percentage of women in their parliaments, and Commonwealth countries as a group have an average of only 13.4 per cent.

- *Local democracy*

Local democracy, particularly the strengthening of elected local government and citizens' participation, is an important way to deepen the democratic process. This can be achieved through careful and well-planned decentralisation that devolves power to local government institutions that are accountable, transparent, representative and adequately financed. Local democracy helps to ensure that individuals living in poverty can be involved in the decisions that affect their lives.

- *Participation*

Political participation must be promoted on a variety of levels. This means more than electing representatives in periodic national elections. It also requires opportunities for direct participation by those most affected by government decisions, particularly the most disadvantaged in any society. This means their involvement in policy formulation, design and delivery of basic services at the local level, and policy monitoring through, for example, participatory budgeting.

- *Civic associations and media and press freedom*

Vibrant civil society organisations (CSOs) and a free press and media can encourage citizens to hold their government to account, promote the representation of disadvantaged groups, enhance tolerance and strengthen the cohesion of diverse and multicultural societies. It is important that both groupings maintain appropriate standards of their own accountability and transparency.

65. Human rights

- *Political and civil rights*

These include the rights typically associated with the International Covenant of Civil and Political Rights, such as permitting free and fair elections and universal suffrage, freedom of association, freedom of speech and information, freedom of movement, equality before the law, due process, *habeas corpus* and general security of the person. An independent, effective, non-corrupt and accessible judicial system is required to protect, respect and fulfil these and other human rights, as is the development of a range of human rights institutions.

- *Social and economic rights*

Such rights include: the right to an adequate standard of living in terms of food, clothing and housing; the right to physical and mental health; the right to education; the right to work; the right to organise and collectively bargain; and the right to social security.

- *Gender rights*

Democratic values also encompass group-specific gender rights to prevent discrimination against women, and to enable them to benefit equitably from all that society has to offer and to participate equally in its governance. Gender rights include, among others, the right to personal security and redress against violence, reproductive health, equal pay for equal work and political representation at all levels. They can be supported through policies and processes such as gender-responsive budgeting and gender mainstreaming. Gender rights also include men's rights not to suffer discrimination and to equity in pro-poor development strategies.

- *Group rights*

Group rights are necessary to protect those, such as indigenous peoples, who may suffer due to their religion, ethnicity or caste. Group rights cover areas such as the right to use indigenous languages in judicial systems, the right to education in one's own language, freedom of worship, special representation rights and the right to maintain, protect and develop land of sacred or historical importance. These group rights help ensure cultural diversity.

66. This perspective on democracy has a number of significant characteristics that set it apart from other approaches to democracy:

- *Reflecting a Commonwealth perspective*

The democratic values reflect and encompass the fundamental political values and commitments of Commonwealth member states expressed in the Harare and Fancourt Declarations. The Harare Declaration emphasises democratic procedures and institutions and the importance of an independent judiciary, the rule of law and just and honest government. It also prioritises respect for human rights and equality for women. The Fancourt Declaration stresses accountability, transparency and the elimination of corruption. In addition, it highlights the importance of participation and civil society, and the need to oppose all forms of discrimination based on ethnicity, gender, race and religion.[8]

- *Embracing human rights*

Many analysts define democracy in a narrow procedural sense, focusing on free and fair elections and the basic political and civil rights required to make these possible. In contrast, this Report's definition is far broader and recognises important contemporary concerns such as local democracy and the full range of human rights.[9] Free and fair elections providing real political choice remain, however, central to any meaningful conception of democracy.

- *Embracing democratic diversity*

It is common to conceive of democracy as uni-dimensional and think that countries can be placed along a single continuum from non-democratic to democratic. This Report's perspective on democracy is multi-dimensional in the sense that it recognises a range of core values, discussed above. While a country may meet democratic requirements with respect to one value, it may be lacking in relation to another. Countries can thus be 'differently democratic'. The Harare Declaration commits the Commonwealth to the protection and promotion of democracy, democratic processes and institutions that reflect national circumstances.

- *Realising democratic values in practice*

Most countries have constitutions specifying democratic principles and have signed international agreements signalling their willingness to adhere to democratic values, particularly human rights. But they fail to realise many of these rights in practice. This Group's perspective on democracy firmly emphasises the importance of a country's practice, not merely its nominal commitments. It considers democracy to be meaningful in people's lives when it is put into practice rather than simply enshrined as constitutional or legal principles.

- *Emphasising interdependent values*

Democratic values are interdependent. For example, realising social and economic rights is necessary for achieving the civil right to equality before the law. In conditions of extreme inequality a poor peasant cannot afford the legal representation to counter a wealthy landowner in a land dispute case, nor would such a person have the education or financial means to run for political office. Similarly, making governments accountable to citizens helps guarantee that the state will uphold human rights. In this sense, realising different democratic values in practice can make them mutually reinforcing.

- *Promoting different arenas of democracy*

Democracy need not be confined to state institutions. This Report's approach to democracy is that democratic values such as accountability and civil rights, as well as economic and social rights, can be promoted in a variety of different arenas, including state institutions (e.g., the school system), international organisations (e.g., the IMF and World Bank), the economic sphere (e.g., transnational corporations), civil society (e.g., non-governmental organisations) and the household. Democratic practices in these different arenas help reinforce one another.[10]

2.3 Making Democracy Work for Pro-Poor Development

67. The global political landscape has changed dramatically in recent decades. Twenty-five years ago there were some 35 democracies in the world, most of them in the wealthy industrialised nations. Today this number has grown to around 130.[11] Many of these new democracies are in Commonwealth countries.

68. Some processes of democratisation, however, have faltered. Despite the long history of democratic governance in some Commonwealth countries, in others there is an urgent need to encourage democratic reforms. A number of Commonwealth countries, for instance, have not established basic democratic procedures such as free and fair multiparty elections. Other countries, both inside and outside the Commonwealth, may have electoral institutions in place but have experienced little change with regard to the respect, protection and fulfilment of many human rights, including civil rights, gender rights and social and economic rights. Economic and political elites have frequently been able to preserve their privileges in the new democratic contexts, often at the expense of the poor. The wave of democratisation that occurred in the last quarter of a century has lost momentum. As the *Human Development Report 2002*, produced by the United Nations Development Programme (UNDP), points out, "the spread of democratisation appears to have stalled, with many countries failing to consolidate and deepen the first steps towards democracy".[12]

69. One of the central problems of these stalled processes of democratisation is institutional weakness. Democratic values cannot be achieved in practice through good intentions alone. Effective institutions are essential for successful democratisation. But many new and fragile democracies seem to lack the institutional infrastructure required to turn democracy into a reality. Some of the necessary institutions include, for example, electoral commissions, ombudsmen, parliamentary oversight committees, highly-trained civil servants in both central and local government, police forces, schools, and accessible and impartial judicial systems that uphold the rule of law and human rights. Free and fair elections, which are central to the democratic process,

require legal and political institutions to ensure freedom of information, speech and political association, and to guarantee a free and independent media. Guidelines for party funding are important to protect the integrity of the political process. Targeted strategies need to be adopted to increase women's representation in parliament and local government, such as setting quotas and leadership training. Internal democracy within parties can also contribute significantly to accountability within political institutions. Institutional mechanisms and appropriate constitutional and legal frameworks are required to check the potential abuse of executive power and to challenge corruption. It is also important that democracy is not reduced merely to majority rule, and there should be effective safeguards for protecting group rights, including the right to dissent.

70. For poor communities to have a voice in making decisions about resource distribution and other issues that affect their lives, there must be mechanisms and institutions that empower these communities, such as participatory budgeting processes.[13] Moreover, an effective public service is essential to help develop and deliver government policies. Successful local democracy requires strengthening the democratic structures and processes of local government. As UNDP recently emphasised: "In the long run building stronger and more accountable local government is the only way to make decentralisation pro-poor. But it requires time, resources and capacity building. For the poor the lasting benefits will outweigh the immediate costs."[14] Promoting local democracy and accountable and transparent decentralisation can also help to reduce the scope of avoidable conflicts.

71. Democracy also requires effective institutions beyond the nation state, at the regional and global level. For instance, international financial institutions such as the World Bank and IMF, and organisations within the United Nations system, need to ensure appropriate multilateral support for democracy in member countries and to themselves embrace institutional mechanisms that permit poor countries and small states to influence decisions.

72. Institution-building at the local, national and international levels is vital to help deepen democracy. These institutions are also necessary to deliver development policies to those people marginalised by poverty. This Report reflects these issues by encouraging wide-ranging forms of institutional development, for example with respect to state administration (Section 4.1) and international economic institutions (Section 5.2).

73. Despite the global wave of democratisation and attempts to build accompanying democratic institutions, the problem of poverty has persisted, both within the Commonwealth and worldwide (see Section 3).[15] This has led some analysts to suggest that democracy is not working effectively for pro-poor development.

74. Is there any concrete evidence that democracy and development reinforce each other? Social scientists have not established an unambiguous and indisputable relationship between the two.[16] While some have found a causal connection or statistical association, their evidence is contested. These diverse results partly reflect differences of method: Social scientists use a variety of definitions and measures of development and democracy; they examine different time periods; or they study different clusters of cases. But the lack of definitive results is also due to history. The rise of democracy in Western Europe in the nineteenth and early twentieth centuries occurred under specific historical conditions, including the growth of a strong manufacturing sector through the industrial revolution, the print revolution and the growth of the print media, the political struggles of well-organised urban workers and women, the waning of the landed aristocracy, and imperial exploitation and domination. Some of these conditions are unlikely to be repeated in the contemporary developing countries of the South. Instead a range of different relationships between development and democracy is evident. In contrast to the Western European experience, some countries, such as Chile and some of the East Asian 'tigers', have experienced economic development under authoritarian regimes. In Latin America in the 1990s, democratisation was associated with increasing disparities in income.

75. The relationship between development and democracy should thus not be oversimplified. The sequencing of reforms, the historical configuration of class relations, state strength and a country's place in the geopolitical context all mediate the development-democracy relationship.

76. Despite these historical variations, however, the Expert Group emphatically supports both democracy and pro-poor development as objectives in their own right, and believes that they can be encouraged to be mutually reinforcing as is envisaged in the Fancourt and Harare Declarations. It is possible to learn from history and challenge the pessimism of those who question the association between development and democracy.

77. How can democracy and development be made to work together? Of the vast range of possible development strategies, some are consistent with democratic values while others have a limited democratic content. An example of the latter kind is top-down development solutions that do not involve consultation with, or participation of, the poor. This Report aims deliberately to focus on the former kind: those development policies that in themselves uphold or promote democratic values. For instance, in one case highlighted in this Report, local participation in creating school curricula has not only promoted development through improved education but at the same time has encouraged democratic participation and accountability at the local level (Box 3). In a different case government budgets have been monitored by women's groups in a process that has not only highlighted the development gaps and gender bias of the

budget but simultaneously encouraged grassroots participation of local people in decision-making and gender rights (Box 1).

78. With these kinds of policies it is possible to make democracy work for pro-poor development. While encouraging development, such policies will simultaneously be strengthening transitions to democracy. As will be discussed below, making democracy work for pro-poor development requires a partnership between the state, the market and civil society.

2.4 The Key Partnership: States, Markets, Civil Society and the International Community

79. This Report argues that the state, the market, civil society and the international community each has a vital role to play in delivering development and democracy. Indeed, it is a mistake to argue for the primacy of any one of these four elements as each is essential. That said, the foundations of democratic development lie in democratic and accountable institutions of government.

States

80. A strong, effective, accountable state is the first pillar of democracy and development. Neither can be imported. International institutions alone cannot and should not take responsibility for eradicating poverty, authoritarianism and conflict. National governments should take the initiative by ensuring that their own core institutions of democracy are fully accountable, and by adopting pro-poor development strategies and promoting democratic reforms and human rights at all levels – in local government, at the national level, and in the international organisations in which they participate.

81. The foundations of a democratic state are worth recalling: a freely and fairly elected parliament that is broadly representative of the people of the country; an executive (government) that is answerable to parliament; an independent judiciary; a police force that responds to the law for its operations and the government for its administration; and armed forces that are answerable to the government and parliament. For democracy to survive and function properly each of these institutions must be held to account. This requires: an independent electoral commission; an independent human rights commission; a freedom of information commission; and an ombudsman. Furthermore, at the heart of democracy and development lie the resources of a nation. It is imperative that parliament is the only channel through which the executive is funded and that the public accounts system be transparent and straightforward, clearly reflecting where money is coming from and where it is going to. The financial affairs of any democratic government should be monitored by

parliament through a public accounts committee, and by an auditor-general answerable to parliament (Section 4.1).

Markets

82. Markets have an essential place in the pursuit of development and democracy. Economic growth fuelled by market competition can contribute to many, if not all, aspects of poverty reduction. Domestic and cross-border private investment provides the majority of resources that currently finance development. The private sector can take up responsibilities as a partner in the quest for pro-poor development and democracy. Codes of corporate governance and practices that demonstrate a respect for democratic institutions and culture, that promote human rights (particularly labour rights), that prohibit corruption and that are properly enforced and monitored by companies are all part of that responsibility (Section 5.1).

Civil society

83. Civil society is the third pillar of pro-poor development and democratisation. Building the capacity of citizens' organisations and a free and well-informed media are critical for promoting citizen participation, holding government to account and empowering poor communities. Poor people and poor communities, for example, are in the best position to understand and articulate their own needs, and their voices should be heard directly within government. Often they are not, however, and here political rights and opportunities can be bolstered through community action. The media plays an important role both in giving voice to citizens and in holding government and the private sector to account on their behalf. The responsibility of civil society is to ensure that their own practices respect democratic values such as tolerance and accountability, and that their actions positively promote pro-poor development and the strengthening of democratic culture (Section 2.2). Equally, the press and media have a responsibility to set high professional standards and to encourage and reward responsible journalism.

The international community

84. Beyond the state, the market and civil society, there is a need for action in the international community. The wealthier industrialised countries must not impede development through their own protectionist measures, including subsidies and restrictions on market access in agriculture and textiles. They must promote and work within a rules-based and transparent multilateral trading system that is more responsive to the needs of poor countries. Having committed themselves to the MDGs and to the New Partnership for Africa's Development (NEPAD), the industrialised countries must now implement their pledges, providing resources in ways that promote

democracy and development. Specifically, this means providing debt relief that releases adequate resources for governments to pursue development programmes, particularly in the areas of health and education, and increasing untied official aid and direct budgetary support to the levels needed to attain the MDGs. Where international economic organisations such as the IMF, the World Bank and the WTO set down conditionality or constraints on policy, it must be in the pursuit of pro-poor development, and must work in ways that do not erode democratic institutions and human rights at the national and sub-national levels (Section 5.2). Finally, in respect of war and armed conflict, when domestic efforts have been made and failed, the international community must take action to reduce conflict and insecurity (Section 5.3).

85. This Report is a call for responsibility and partnership – from governments, from firms, from civil society and from the international community. Without responsibility on all these levels, development and democracy will remain rhetoric rather than become reality.

3
Poverty in the Commonwealth

86. This section focuses on poverty in the Commonwealth and the progress of Commonwealth countries towards achieving the Millennium Development Goals (MDGs). It highlights the severe deprivation that exists in the Commonwealth that requires urgent action by Commonwealth Heads of Government and the international community.

87. The problem of global poverty hardly needs restating. The statistics are all too clear and the personal stories overwhelming. With around 1.2 billion people living on less than one dollar a day and 2.8 billion on under two dollars a day, there are no grounds for complacency.[17] And global income inequality is rising. According to the World Bank's *World Development Report 2003*: "average income in the wealthiest 20 countries is 37 times that in the poorest 20 countries – twice the ratio in 1970".[18] Moreover, 60 countries finished the decade of the 1990s with lower per capita incomes than at its beginning.[19] But what do such general facts and statements mean for the Commonwealth?

88. A recent report vividly demonstrates the importance of reducing poverty in the Commonwealth and of action by Commonwealth member states both individually and collectively:[20]

- One third of the Commonwealth's two billion people live on less than one dollar a day and 64 per cent on less than two dollars a day.

- Around 60 per cent of global HIV cases are in the Commonwealth, and four of the nine most affected countries are Commonwealth members. Nearly 60 per cent of Commonwealth citizens lack access to essential drugs and adequate sanitation facilities.

- Some 270 million people in the Commonwealth lack access to improved water supplies.

- Women constitute around 70 per cent of those living in poverty in the Commonwealth. Women are discriminated against in much of the Commonwealth in areas ranging from unequal pay for equal work to customary inheritance and marriage regimes, in addition to suffering domestic violence.

- Around half of the world's 300 million indigenous peoples live in the Commonwealth, and they frequently suffer discrimination, intolerance, prejudice and violation of their land rights.[21]

- Around half of the world's 115 million children without access to primary school live in the Commonwealth.

- Young people constitute over 50 per cent of the Commonwealth population. A large percentage of them are adversely affected by unemployment, poverty, HIV/AIDS and illiteracy.

89. This list could go on and detail particular cases and stories in Commonwealth countries of, for instance, exploitative child labour or comparatively low life expectancy among indigenous peoples. It could also highlight the special problems facing those living in the 32 small states of the Commonwealth. The message should by now be clear: Poverty in all its dimensions is a special challenge throughout the countries of the Commonwealth and for the Commonwealth as a whole.

90. Another way of thinking about poverty in the Commonwealth is to assess members' likelihood of achieving the MDGs, adopted by world leaders at the UN General Assembly in September 2000. Each of the eight Goals is accompanied by targets to be achieved by 2015 (see Appendix B). The Goals are to: (1) eradicate extreme poverty and hunger; (2) achieve universal primary education; (3) promote gender equality and empower women; (4) reduce child mortality; (5) improve maternal health; (6) combat HIV/AIDS, malaria and other diseases; (7) ensure environmental sustainability; and (8) develop a global partnership for development.

91. The UNDP's *Human Development Report 2003* reviews progress towards the MDGs and provides an assessment of which countries require priority attention with respect to the achievement of each Goal and to the Goals overall. Progress is classified as slow, moderate or fast, and priority status as top priority, high priority or low priority. Top priority countries for each Goal have extreme human poverty in that Goal combined with slow or even reversing progress towards it. It is on such countries, argues UNDP, that the world's attention and resources must be focused. A country is designated high priority for a Goal if it has both extreme human poverty in that Goal and moderate progress towards it or if it has medium human poverty in that Goal and slow progress towards it.

92. Table 1 shows those Commonwealth countries that are designated top priority and high priority for each of the MDGs. Table 2 depicts which Commonwealth countries are top priority, high priority and low priority across all the Goals.[22] It is clear that progress towards the MDGs for Commonwealth countries is extremely mixed:

Table 1: Priority Status for Specific Millennium Development Goals in Commonwealth Countries

Goal	Target	Indicator	Top priority countries	High priority countries
Goal 1: Eradicate extreme poverty and hunger	Halve the proportion of people living on under $1 a day	Population living below $1 a day (%)	Cameroon, The Gambia, Kenya, Nigeria, Sierra Leone, Solomon Islands, United Republic of Tanzania, Vanuatu, Zambia, Zimbabwe	Jamaica, Pakistan, Papua New Guinea, Saint Lucia, Swaziland
	Halve the proportion of people suffering from hunger	Undernourished people (% population)	Bangladesh, Kenya, Lesotho, Papua New Guinea, Sierra Leone, United Republic of Tanzania, Zambia	Botswana, The Gambia, India, Swaziland, Trinidad and Tobago, Zimbabwe
Goal 2: Achieve universal primary education	Ensure that all children can complete primary education	Net primary enrolment ratio (%)	Mozambique, United Republic of Tanzania	The Bahamas, Botswana, The Gambia, Namibia, South Africa
Goal 3: Promote gender equality and empower women	Eliminate gender disparity in all levels of education by 2005	Ratio of girls to boys in primary and secondary education (%)	Mozambique, Sierra Leone	Cameroon, India
Goal 4: Reduce child mortality	Reduce under-five infant mortality rates by two thirds	Under-five mortality rate (per 1000 live births)	Botswana, Cameroon, Kenya, Lesotho, Nigeria, Sierra Leone, Swaziland, United Republic of Tanzania, Zambia, Zimbabwe	Gambia, Malawi, Mozambique, Pakistan, Papua New Guinea, South Africa, Uganda
Goal 7: Ensure environmental sustainability	Halve the proportion of people without sustainable access to safe drinking water	People with access to improved water sources (%)	Papua New Guinea	Cameroon, Malawi, Namibia, Nigeria, South Africa, Uganda
	Achieve a significant improvement in the lives of at least 100m slum dwellers	People with access to adequate sanitation (%)	Cameroon, Nigeria	Bangladesh, Botswana, India, Malawi, Namibia, Papua New Guinea, South Africa, Zimbabwe

Table 2: Priority Status across all the Millennium Development Goals in Commonwealth Countries

Priority status	Country	Number of Commonwealth countries in category out of world total
Top priority	Cameroon, Kenya, Lesotho, Mozambique, Nigeria, Sierra Leone, United Republic of Tanzania, Zambia, Zimbabwe	9 out of 31
High priority	The Bahamas, Botswana, The Gambia, India, Malawi, Namibia, Papua New Guinea, South Africa, Swaziland	9 out of 28
Low priority	Australia, Bangladesh, Barbados, Belize, Canada, Cyprus, Fiji Islands, Ghana, Guyana, Jamaica, Malaysia, Malta, Mauritius, New Zealand, Pakistan, Saint Lucia, Samoa, Singapore, Sri Lanka, Trinidad and Tobago, Uganda, United Kingdom, Vanuatu	23 out of 78
Insufficient data	Antigua and Barbuda, Brunei Darussalam, Dominica, Grenada, Kiribati, Maldives, Nauru, Saint Kitts and Nevis, Saint Vincent and the Grenadines, Seychelles, Solomon Islands, Tonga, Tuvalu	13 out of 32

Note: *Top priority* countries across the Goals means that they are top priority countries for at least three Goals or for at least half of the Goals for which they have data, with a minimum of three data points. If data are available for only two Goals they are top priority for both. *High priority* countries across the Goals do not fall into the top priority category but are top or high priority for at least three Goals, are top priority for two Goals, or are top or high priority for at least half of the Goals for which they have data, with a minimum of three data points. If data are available for only two Goals, they are top or high priority in both. *Low priority* countries are those with sufficient data to be assessed and that do not fall into either the top or high priority categories.

- Of the 31 overall top priority countries, nine are from the Commonwealth: Cameroon, Kenya, Lesotho, Mozambique, Nigeria, Sierra Leone, United Republic of Tanzania, Zambia and Zimbabwe.

- 10 Commonwealth countries are designated top priority with respect to the target of halving the proportion of people living on under $1 a day.

- 17 Commonwealth countries are classified as either top or high priority for the Goal of reducing child mortality.

- Several Commonwealth countries have made significant progress towards the MDGs. For instance, 11 countries in the Commonwealth have made fast progress towards the goal of halving the number of people who suffer from hunger by 2015.

93. The lack of progress of many Commonwealth countries towards achieving the MDGs is extremely worrying. It would undoubtedly appear even worse were it possible to obtain data for the full range of Goals and for all Commonwealth member states. There are not sufficient data to make reliable progress assessments respecting the targets for Goals 5 and 6. Additionally, the indicators used for other targets are variable in their country coverage. In particular, for 13 small Commonwealth states there are insufficient data to assess their overall priority status across all the MDGs (Table 2). It is clearly important to build greater statistical capacity in these states.[23]

4
National Measures to Support Development and Democracy

94. Any serious attempt to understand how to make democracy work for pro-poor development cannot simply sketch out the problem of poverty, as has been done above, but must be more specific about the particular national obstacles to development faced by poor countries. The Expert Group has identified a number of key areas in which there are severe obstacles to pro-poor development: state administration and corruption, macroeconomic policy, education, health, environment, land, infrastructure and new technologies. It is essential for national governments to undertake reforms in these areas, in partnership with the market, civil society and the international community, to promote pro-poor development. The Group recognises that some of the most significant contemporary challenges for developing countries, such as the HIV/AIDS pandemic and environmental degradation, did not confront present day industrialised countries or the Newly Industrialising Countries (NICs).

4.1 State Administration

95. Poor states often have weak administrative capacity. This is particularly the case in newly emerging and fragile democracies, small states and countries recovering from conflict. Public officials may be poorly trained or lack experience in public expenditure management. Low pay for civil servants contributes to the lack of high quality administrators and poor morale in many developing countries. Furthermore, the disparity in remuneration of local officials and foreign-funded consultants exacerbates the problem of low motivation. In addition, state institutions, such as government ministries or judiciaries, may lack sufficient resources or be plagued by entrenched systems of corruption. Inadequate numbers of women at decision-making levels in the civil service and judiciary means that women's interests are not represented in policy formulation and implementation. Such problems can not only exist at the national level but also extend to the provincial and district levels.[24] Institutional reforms at the international level, although essential to democracy and development (Section 5), are unlikely to 'trickle down' to the national and sub-national levels. The problems of ensuring effective state administration and tackling corruption must be tackled directly.

96. Ineffective state administration, which should be understood as a failure of good governance, can cause major problems for development. A government might have well-intentioned pro-poor economic and social policies, but not have the administrative experience to target those most in need; it might receive substantial overseas

development aid, but not have the capacity to deliver aid programmes at the local level or to outlying regions, and may have to contend with corrupt bureaucrats who siphon off the funds. Poor administrative capacity also affects the ability of countries to absorb the foreign aid committed to them, which is reflected in low disbursement ratios. As former Indian Prime Minister Rajiv Gandhi once lamented, only 17 per cent of development funding in some of the states in India actually reached the poor. Despite pressures to cut back the size and functions of the state, there remains the crucial task of building effective state administration to help create, implement and monitor pro-poor development strategies. Several key steps can be taken in this regard.

97. The government's budget is a key instrument for determining the overall trajectory of development and for promoting efficiency and equity as a means of building stable, cohesive societies. In many countries it is the main source of macroeconomic instability and there is often a significant disjuncture between budgetary expenditures and pro-poor outcomes. It is crucial that expenditure management systems are strengthened to ensure accountability, transparency and equity; that budgetary processes involve early consultations to increase responsiveness to local needs; and that monitoring and evaluation mechanisms are strengthened to improve compliance and the impact of budgets on disadvantaged groups such as women, children and youth.

98. In most Commonwealth countries audit reports are not used by parliaments as the basis for calling government ministers and officials to account for their revealed performance failures or maladministration. Moreover, in many instances such reports are not completed on a timely basis. However, in Uganda not only does the Public Accounts Committee scrutinise and comment on the Auditor-General's reports, but MPs, in general, are becoming increasingly interested in public sector performance. Changes are also occurring in this area in Ghana. High priority should be attached to the timely completion of the auditor-general's (or equivalent) reports and they should be used to strengthen the role of parliament, particularly the public accounts committee (or equivalent bodies), in holding governments to account on budgetary expenditure. Policies to tackle corruption, such as creating parliamentary oversight mechanisms or ombudsmen, not only serve to enhance the state's administrative capabilities, but also promote the democratic values of accountability and transparency.

99. Building civil service capacity can help deliver pro-poor policies in areas such as health and education, thereby ensuring effective state administration and upholding social and economic rights. In South Africa, the Commonwealth recently developed a programme for the Cabinet Office of the Presidency and the nine Provincial Executive Council Offices, aimed at enhancing policy analysis capacity and improving procedures and co-ordination skills. Training civil servants in gender planning and gender-responsive budgeting can not only improve the targeting of anti-poverty

Box 1: Introducing Gender-Responsive Budgeting in South Africa

South Africa has been the site of innovative public sector reform in the area of gender-responsive budgeting (sometimes known as 'women's budgets'). Gender-responsive budgets are allocations of public spending that take account of a gender perspective to ensure that a government's international and national commitments to achieve gender equality goals, such as in work or education, are reflected in resource allocation. There are now similar initiatives in over 40 countries, supported and networked by organisations led by the Commonwealth Secretariat, United Nations Development Fund for Women (UNIFEM) and International Development Research Centre (IDRC). At their meeting in London (September 2002), Commonwealth Finance Ministers agreed to review progress made in this area in their countries in 2005. The South African women's budget initiative, which began in the mid-1990s, contains two elements. First is a process largely 'outside' government, in which non-governmental organisations (in collaboration with parliamentarians) monitor and critique the gender sensitivity of budgetary allocations. This process attempts to involve citizen participation in the area of budgets, from which many people – especially from disadvantaged social groups – have long been excluded. The second element is a government initiative co-ordinated by the Finance Ministry to undertake gender analysis of the budget. This serves as one of the Commonwealth Secretariat's pilot projects to engender macroeconomic policy-making.

Perhaps the most visible result of the 'inside' government initiative has been the inclusion of discussion of gender issues in documents tabled on budget day in 1998 and 1999. These discussions were published within the documents, rather than separately, in order to promote recognition that gender is a mainstream issue. Another significant result concerns the medium-term expenditure framework (MTEF). The Department of Finance has accepted that the money amounts, in addition to physical outputs and outcomes, be disaggregated by a number of factors including gender.

The introduction of gender-responsive budgeting is a means of ensuring effective state administration, which is a major challenge for pro-poor development. The gender initiatives have served to deepen democracy, in the sense that they promote democratic values such as accountability, participation, gender rights and a vibrant civil society. They show how democracy can work for pro-poor development.

Note: The case material on South Africa draws on Budlender 2000, and Budlender, Hicks and Vetten 2002. See also UNDP 2002, 80 and Rao 2002, para. 105.

programmes but also contribute to promoting gender rights.

100. Strong democratic institutions can be the bedrock of effective state administration. Developing effective mechanisms for the involvement of poor communities in policy decisions on aid programmes increases the state's administrative capabilities while at the same time advancing the democratic values of participation and local democracy. Judicial reforms can enhance the legal system's ability to enforce minimum wage legislation or laws concerning land access, promote equality before the law and greater balance of power between different branches of the state, and also tackle corruption. Ensuring a free and independent media helps reinforce accountability and transparency of government institutions.

101. Strategies such as these, of which there are many more, help make democracy work to improve state administration, and thereby promote pro-poor development. But can such strategies be made to work in the real world? Two inspiring examples of this approach being successfully put into practice are the development of gender-sensitive budgeting in South Africa (Box 1) and the struggle against government corruption in the Indian state of Rajasthan (Box 2).

4.2 Pro-Poor Economic and Social Policies

Macroeconomic policy

102. Macroeconomic instability in poor countries has proved problematic for the pursuit of pro-poor development. Inflation, fuelled by weak policies, is a highly regressive implicit tax on the poor, for they usually do not own assets whose appreciation acts as a hedge against price increases. Equally, loose policies lead to balance of payments crises that necessitate stabilisation programmes, which tend to have a disproportionately adverse impact on the poor. Unsustainable budget deficits are the main source of instability in many countries and are often caused by unfundable populist expenditures. Macroeconomic instability also encourages capital flight.

103. A stable macroeconomic environment is a necessary condition for effective pro-poor development policies. Governments must make efforts to avoid policies that increase inflation, contribute to balance of payments crises and create unsustainable budget deficits. Welfare programmes and safety nets should be well targeted. Governments should also attempt to create macroeconomic stability to attract foreign capital (Section 5.1). Financial stability can additionally help create an environment in which small firms and family businesses in developing countries are stimulated to innovate.[25] Tax reforms, particularly improvements in tax administration, are required to help generate the financial resources necessary to implement pro-poor development strategies. It is similarly important to promote the efficiency of public

Box 2: Organising against Government Corruption in India

The Commonwealth Human Rights Initiative has recently documented an important example of grassroots struggle against government corruption in India. In many Indian regions government development projects – such as building schools, dispensaries, roads, community centres and residential quarters – frequently appear to have been completed on paper but have not been undertaken in reality. A major reason is corruption among local public officials who make false receipts and issue bogus reports for such projects, while appropriating the earmarked funds for themselves. Local communities find it difficult to hold these officials to account because public expenditure records remain largely secret: Poor villagers have no right to ask for detailed expenditure information.

One response to this problem of corrupt and ineffective state administration has been the Right to Information Movement in the state of Rajasthan, spearheaded since the mid-1990s by the Mazdoor Kisan Shakti Sangathan (MKSS – Workers and Farmers Power Organisation), a grassroots organisation of mainly poor people from socially excluded groups. The MKSS strategy has two main elements. First, they have undertaken large-scale public protests against local and state government with the objective of obtaining legislative and regulatory reforms that provide a legal basis for local efforts to obtain official expenditure records. The second element is locally organised 'jan sunwais' – or public hearings – at which expenditure statements derived from official records are read aloud to assembled villagers in order to help uncover corrupt practices.

Based on the principle of collective and local verification of accounts, the campaign has had important successes. The movement has not only exposed fraud in local government but also on a number of occasions local officials, humiliated by the public hearings, have returned embezzled public funds. The MKSS's collective process has deterred further corruption and generated a wider campaign for legislative and regulatory change at the state and national level.

The campaign in Rajasthan has contributed to more effective state administration and the fight against corruption, enhancing the possibilities for development policies to reach disadvantaged populations. But it also shows how democracy can be made to work for pro-poor development, as the MKSS strategy involves processes of accountability, local participation, the involvement of civic associations, local democracy and the political right to information.

Note: The discussion on Rajasthan uses analyses from Commonwealth Human Rights Initiative 2001, 84, Jenkins and Goetz 1999 and Roy 2000.

enterprises as well as the implementation of pro-market reforms and deregulation of economic processes as a means of generating resources for development.

104. Economic reform programmes adopted by many countries to achieve macro-economic stabilisation and effect structural reforms, involving liberalisation and deregulation, are associated with significant transitional costs that generally hit the poor more than other social groups. It is important that these reforms are supported by the creation of safety nets to address these costs. Safety nets not only provide social protection but also create a more conducive environment for effecting reforms that are necessary to improve the competitiveness of economies in the face of globalisation.

105. The challenge for governments is also to implement development policies that simultaneously promote and uphold democratic values. This requires specific priorities in the areas of education, health, environment, land and infrastructure.

Education

106. Education is a basic right of all human beings. It is also one of the most essential prerequisites for successful integration into the global economy in the twenty-first century. Human capital is a critical asset for development, and the problem of skills shortage in the developing world is acute. Education for girl children can have a profound impact on political freedom, gender equality, income poverty reduction, effective population policies and family health.[26] Yet as noted in the previous section, millions of children around the world do not have access to basic education, and most of these are in poor countries in the South, including in Commonwealth countries.

107. If poor individuals and communities are to participate in development and benefit from globalisation, education must become central to government poverty alleviation strategies. Education policy, however, is still often seen as peripheral and some governments in South Asia and Africa continue to spend more on arms than on primary education services. The international community has also failed to live up to their commitments made in the Dakar Declaration on Education for All.

108. Education policy should be encouraged to incorporate democratic values. Educational reforms that involve local communities in designing curricula or managing schools, for instance, can both contribute to pro-poor development and encourage the democratic values of participation and local democracy. An example of how this has occurred through community schools in Egypt is discussed in Box 3.

Health

109. The statistics in Section 3 demonstrate an acute global failure to respect,

Box 3: Promoting Participation through Community Schools in Egypt

Among the many inspiring examples of pro-poor national economic and social policy with a high democratic content is the Community Schools Project in Egypt discussed in a recent report by Oxfam. Around 30 million Egyptian adults are illiterate and the number of girls out of school is estimated at around one million. In 1992 the Ministry of Education, together with UNICEF, piloted a community school model in four of Upper Egypt's most remote rural hamlets, aiming to provide universal access to primary schooling, with a focus on girls' enrolment. The Government was responsible for financing teachers' salaries, books and school nutrition programmes. The local community was to provide premises, form an education committee to manage the school, and advise on the curriculum. Village education committees were to select local women for teacher training. Finally, UNICEF was to train staff and provide furniture and equipment.

Within a four-year period it was clear that the community schools, of which there were eventually 125, were performing more successfully than the formal education system in reaching marginalised and remote communities. In some hamlets enrolment rates for girls increased from 15 per cent to over 70 per cent. Pupils in the pilot schools were as much as three times more successful in passing government tests than their state school counterparts, and the community schools also provided adult literacy classes.

The schools demonstrated how democratic values can work for pro-poor development in the area of national economic and social policy. The structure and processes of the project had a strong democratic element. Through encouraging local community involvement, the schools promoted the democratic values of participation and local democracy. The project also had a substantial gender rights component. In addition, the co-ordination between local villages, the national government and UNICEF facilitated accountability of the state and an international agency to local community needs. Democracy and development were closely intertwined.

Note: See Watkins 2000, 325-327.

protect and fulfil the right to health. Like education, health is not only a right, but also closely related to development issues. Ill-health remains a major consequence of poverty: Due to a lack of access to clean water, adequate nutrition and medical care, poor people (especially children and women) are more susceptible to infectious diseases than most other social groups.

110. Ill-health is also a cause of poverty. A single experience of sickness in a family can divert energy and resources, leaving the household in deep poverty. Diseases such as malaria, tuberculosis and HIV/AIDS are not only personal tragedies; a high prevalence of such diseases is associated with significant reductions in economic growth. The threat is especially great in sub-Saharan Africa, home to two thirds of the world's 33 million sufferers from HIV/AIDS. By 2020 more than 25 per cent of the workforce in some countries might be lost to AIDS.[27] HIV/AIDS is having a severe effect on public service workers in sub-Saharan Africa, thereby eroding the ability of state institutions to deliver pro-poor policies.

111. The creation of adequate health systems requires not only reforms at the national level but interpretation and implementation of the recent trade-related aspects of intellectual property rights (TRIPS) agreement on affordable drugs in a manner that makes cheap drugs available to poor countries (Section 5.1). Another health issue with international dimensions is the general outflow of trained health workers from developing countries to the more developed ones. Such outflow puts pressure on the governments of the 'source' countries that require these skilled persons to meet the legitimate health care needs of the population. The outflow of skilled workers constitutes a substantial capital transfer from the tax payers of developing countries to the wealthy economies in the North. Recently, concerns have arisen about the UK recruiting nurses and teachers from the Caribbean and elsewhere. The Commonwealth is working to develop best practice in this area. This issue is expected to be addressed at the Commonwealth Education Ministers meeting in Edinburgh this year.

Environment

112. Environmental degradation and poverty are closely interlinked. Poor countries are forced to meet the costs of environmental damage arising not only from domestic sources but from industrialised countries, as is the case with greenhouse gas emissions. Small island states, many of which are Commonwealth members, are threatened by the prospect of sea-level rises linked to global warming, and changing weather patterns can have disastrous consequences for agriculture-dependent countries. Mechanisms for environmental disaster management are often inadequate and under-funded. Governments fail to enforce environmental laws, such as those concerning industrial pollution. In addition it is the poor, such as rural and urban slum

dwellers without access to safe drinking water, or farmers on fragile land, who suffer most from the problems of environmental degradation.

113. Environmental planning that involves consultation with those affected by infrastructure projects promotes accountability to citizens, thereby making democracy work for pro-poor development. In addition, enforcing environmental legislation, such as that related to the dumping of toxic waste, is a fundamental aspect of upholding the rule of law. Governments should also put more expertise and resources into sustainable development projects.[28] The World Summit on Sustainable Development (WSSD) in Johannesburg in August-September 2002 saw important advances, such as China and Canada agreeing to ratify the Kyoto Protocol on greenhouse gases. Yet there remain major problems, such as the failure of the United States – which produces one quarter of all greenhouse gas emissions – to sign the Protocol. Opportunities should be taken to promote 'Type 2' Partnerships developed in the context of the WSSD. Special attention must be given to the environmental problems faced by all, especially small states. The Commonwealth has, for example, recently developed programmes for improved water resource management in nine small states.[29]

Land

114. Access to land, and effective systems of property titling and registration, are widely accepted as essential to development. Land can be a source of life, livelihood and income. This was recognised in the Kingstown Declaration on Land and Development made by Commonwealth Law Ministers in November 2002. Land has been unable to play its full role in development due to a number of problems existing in developing countries: weak institutions that result in inefficient land administration; lack of management and use of customary land that, although an abundant asset for poor people in many countries, remains unproductive and valueless as security for capital because of prohibiting legislation; lack of secure land rights for informal urban communities; lack of equitable access to land for women; and limits on the right of indigenous peoples to own, develop, control and use their lands and territories.

115. Legal and judicial frameworks must adapt to confront these problems. Increased security of tenure provides incentives to invest time, labour and capital. In addition, titled land can be used as collateral to secure credit for investment, while titling also facilitates land transfers, leading to a more productive use of resources.[30] Land reform policies, while having the potential to promote pro-poor development, must always respect democratic processes and the rule of law and avoid discrimination. Land and other social and economic policies can be directed at challenging discrimination against disadvantaged groups, such as Dalits in India and indigenous peoples even in developed Commonwealth countries, thereby encouraging

democratic equality in addition to development. Policies that permit indigenous peoples to own, develop, control and use their lands help secure group rights.

Infrastructure

116. Efficient infrastructure is a key determinant of development prospects. High priority should be attached to infrastructure development that transforms the lives of the poor. This includes roads that link rural communities to markets; irrigation schemes that benefit subsistence farmers; rural electrification; and clean water and sanitation for the urban poor. Addressing these issues will help deliver economic and social rights.

New technologies

117. New technologies have the potential to enhance the capabilities of poor people. But the technological divide between developed and developing countries remains acute. For instance, the cost of Internet access is prohibitively high in many poor countries: While the cost in the US is 1.2 per cent of average monthly income, in Uganda it is 107 per cent.[31] The Internet and other new technologies cannot work for the poor without concerted government effort, in partnership with the private sector, to help bridge the technological divide not only between North and South, but within developing countries themselves.

Capacity and co-ordination

118. It is also essential to politically empower the poor to help them confront the challenges of development. Building the capacity of civil society and associations of the poor, and subsequent strengthening of co-ordination between organisations of the poor and government policy makers, can give poor communities a foundation in their struggle for human rights that allows them to voice their concerns and participate in developing and monitoring pro-poor policies.[32]

119. Developing country governments must co-ordinate their actions with the international community and vice-versa. Implementing pro-poor national economic and social policy in the areas of education, HIV/AIDS or environmental degradation will benefit from complementary action at the international level, such as financing national policies through adequate levels of concessional funding. Similarly, anti-corruption measures at the national level that improve state administration will be more successful if accompanied by effective international action against corruption at the supply end.

120. These general suggestions from the Expert Group to help governments

confront the obstacles to pro-poor development that exist at the national and subnational levels have crystallised into a number of policy recommendations, specified below, to promote pro-poor development and deepen democracy. For national measures to be effective in making development and democracy mutually reinforcing, all Commonwealth governments should commit to ensuring that core institutions exist in their own countries and are fully held to account. These institutions are identified in the recommendations below.

121. The obstacles to development do not, however, only exist on the national level. Some of the most severe impediments to development are at the international level, largely out of the control of most individual developing countries. These impediments, discussed in Section 5, include problems such as the asymmetries of the international trading system, ineffective and inadequate volumes of foreign aid, unstable private capital flows, the policies and programmes of international economic institutions, and international conflict and insecurity.

4.3 Recommended Actions at the National Level

Democratic accountability of government revenue and expenditure

122. Government revenue and expenditure lie at the heart of both democracy and development policy. The Expert Group recognises that a sound and accountable system for drawing up budgets, implementing them and monitoring their impact is a key instrument for promoting pro-poor development and democracy, and for building stable, cohesive societies.

123. Throughout the Commonwealth this requires member governments to commit:

(i) to creating budgetary processes that involve broad citizen consultation and participation on key issues, and to developing procedures for evaluating the impact of budgets on disadvantaged groups such as poor communities, women, children and youth;

(ii) to implementing sound and rigorous government expenditure management systems;

(iii) to improving accountability of budget implementation by ensuring:

(a) that auditors-general (or their equivalents) report to parliament in a timely way and that their reports are made public;

(b) that public accounts committees (or equivalent bodies with oversight of government expenditure) are empowered to summon and question all members of government, and that their reports and hearings are public; and

(iv) to challenging corruption (see below).

124 In supporting these commitments at the intergovernmental level, it would be useful for Commonwealth Heads of Government to request the Secretary-General to establish a technical group to draw up Commonwealth codes of good practice on budgetary processes, expenditure management systems and the oversight and accountability of the budget, and to encourage Commonwealth governments to properly monitor and enforce these codes. In addition, the public needs to understand the budget in order to hold government to account. The Commonwealth Secretariat should also develop a template to facilitate this.

Resources for pro-poor development at the national level

125. The success of the above policies will be enhanced by generating more resources for pro-poor development. To do so, Commonwealth governments need to commit:

(i) to introducing tax reforms, particularly improvements in tax administration, that generate these resources; and

(ii) to promoting the efficiency of public enterprises as well as implementation of pro-market reforms and deregulation of economic processes.

126. The Group stresses that the creation of safety nets should be an integral component of economic liberalisation programmes, to ensure that transitional costs are not borne disproportionately by the most vulnerable groups in society.

127. A greater proportion of resources should be allocated to environmental protection measures, in particular to the prevention of land and water degradation that affect the livelihoods of millions of poor people living on the edge of subsistence.

Committing to core democratic institutions and a strong democratic culture

128. All Commonwealth governments should commit to ensure that the core institutions of democracy exist in their own countries and are fully held to account. Commonwealth Heads of Government could commit to the ten institutions listed below and request the Secretary-General to ensure that these commitments are recorded and monitored regularly.

- A freely and fairly elected **parliament** that is broadly representative of the people of the country, and whose election is overseen by an independent electoral commission.

- An **executive** (government) that is answerable to – and funded solely through – the parliament.

- An independent **judiciary** (which means that judges must be financially secure during the period of their appointment and in retirement).

- A transparent and straightforward **public accounts system** (which clearly reflects where money is coming from and where it is going to) and a **public accounts committee** responsible for monitoring public expenditure.

- An **auditor-general** answerable to parliament (i.e. the public accounts committee) ensuring, *inter alia*, the financial accountability of the executive.

- An independent **human rights commission** that protects citizens from discrimination and human rights abuses and ensures that the government treats all citizens equally.

- A **freedom of information commission** that enables the public to gain access to information about executive decisions and allows individuals to access information held about them by the police and public bodies.

- An **ombudsman**.

- A **police force** that responds to the law for its operations and the government for its administration.

- **Armed forces** that are answerable to the government and parliament, not to political parties, and are responsible for the defence of the country.

129. The Group believes that local democracy, particularly the strengthening of elected local government and wide citizens' participation, including that of women and youth, is an important way to promote democratic values and deepen the democratic process. This can be achieved through careful and well-planned decentralisation that devolves power to local government institutions that are accountable, transparent and representative. To this end, Commonwealth governments can deepen democracy by providing the necessary financial resources to ensure that public sector decentralisation is viable and that local government is able to contribute effectively to the realisation of the MDGs.

130. At every level democracy must be buttressed by a strong democratic culture that respects the full range of social and economic rights, gender rights and group rights. The Commonwealth could and should be a positive force for celebrating cultural diversity and resisting the advance of fundamentalism and intolerance in every member country. Equally important is freedom of information and the freedom of the press and media. In this regard, Commonwealth governments need to commit:

1. to encouraging freedom of the press and media;

2. to promoting training for journalists that encourages responsible journalism, respect for democratic institutions and human rights, and religious and ethnic tolerance; and

3. to strengthening mechanisms to monitor press freedom throughout the Commonwealth.

131. Given the Commonwealth's experience of handling diversity, the Commonwealth Secretariat should seek to convey the positive aspects of cultural diversity, particularly in contexts where it has been negatively exploited to a divisive end, and demonstrate best practice.

132. Commonwealth countries should adopt concrete strategies to achieve the target set by Heads of Government of 30 per cent of women in decision-making, particularly in cabinet, parliament, the public service and local government.

133. The Expert Group recognises the comparative advantage that the Commonwealth has in promoting democratic structures and values and calls upon Heads of Government to increase the capacity of the Commonwealth Secretariat's programmes in this area. In doing so they recognise that the trust enjoyed by the Commonwealth, which is the basis of its comparative advantage in its political work, has been gained by the association's capacity to empathise with the development concerns of its developing country members. It is important, therefore, to increase capacity in the democratisation area without diminishing the ability of the Commonwealth to respond to the development needs of its members, that is, through additional resources, including through a Special Fund for democratisation activities.

Tackling corruption

134. At the national level throughout the Commonwealth, corruption and the looting of public funds should be tackled (as highlighted in the Report of the Commonwealth Expert Group on Good Governance and the Elimination of Corruption). Within national systems, Commonwealth governments can set core

standards in respect of political party financing and codes of ethics and transparency regarding the interests of parliamentarians. At the international level, Commonwealth governments can promote transparency in the contracts between governments and corporations in extractive industries (as is advocated in the present Extractive Industries Transparency Initiative being promulgated by the UK Department for International Development). Finally, all Commonwealth governments need to actively aid fellow Commonwealth countries in the repatriation of illegally acquired public funds and assets that have been transferred abroad. Such aid should include the establishment of appropriate legal frameworks and exploring the possibility of an international convention. The Expert Group believes that a Commonwealth Technical Working Group to examine the issues involved would help advance effective action in this area.

5
International Measures to Promote Development and Democracy

135. Although action at the national level is essential to make democracy work for pro-poor development, some of the most significant obstacles to development exist at the international level and must be addressed in a co-ordinated fashion by the international community. This section explores, first, problems associated with the global economy, including the asymmetries of the international trade regime, unstable private capital flows, unsustainable debt repayments and ineffective international aid (Section 5.1). It then focuses on the policies and procedures of international institutions such as the International Monetary Fund (IMF) and World Bank (Section 5.2). Finally, it describes the obstacles to the pursuit of development and democracy posed by conflict and insecurity (Section 5.3). Each section not only analyses the problems, but also suggests strategies to make democracy work for pro-poor development.

136. The Expert Group's policy recommendations at the international level are designed to encourage Commonwealth Heads of Government and the international community to undertake reforms in these three areas (Section 5.4). The obstacles to pro-poor development are interdependent. Rather than confronting them in isolation, governments and the international community should treat them in an integrated and holistic manner.

5.1 The Global Economy

The international trade regime

137. Trade liberalisation and export-led growth have the potential to bring millions of people out of poverty. If developing countries increased their share of world exports by 5 per cent, this could generate $350 billion, around seven times the amount they receive in aid.[33] The unprecedented success in reducing poverty in East and South-East Asia has been driven by rapid growth in international trade, which was enabled by a concentration on building capacity through education and skills enhancement as well as stability and predictability in economic policy and the political environment.

138. The difficulty for many developing countries is that the current international trade system generates asymmetrical outcomes, making the potential benefits hard to obtain. Wealthier industrialised countries have been the main beneficiaries of trade

liberalisation. The Expert Group believes that creating a transparent rules-based multilateral trading system is an urgent priority for fostering both development and democracy.

139. There are four main problems with the existing trade regime. First, trade liberalisation has a number of short- and medium-term costs that must be minimised in order for developing countries to take full advantage of the benefits of trade. Among these costs has been greater food insecurity as local production declines in the face of foreign competition (often heavily subsidised) and food import bills increase. This occurred in large parts of sub-Saharan Africa and Peru in the 1990s due to rapid liberalisation.[34] Trade liberalisation can have an adverse impact on budgets due to the revenue effect of decreased tariffs, and dumping and over-abundance of cheap imports, especially agricultural products. A World Bank study estimated that sub-Saharan Africa, the world's poorest region, would lose 2 per cent of its income following the Uruguay Round of trade negotiations.[35] Trade liberalisation has had its greatest impact on development in middle-income developing countries rather than in least developed countries. Trade liberalisation is also associated with specific gender opportunities, constraints and challenges. For example, women workers in labour-intensive jobs at the end of global supply chains have suffered from precarious employment and inadequate enforcement of national and international labour standards.

140. The transition costs can be minimised through the appropriate pacing and sequencing of liberalisation. Economic development in the North in the nineteenth and twentieth centuries generally occurred in conditions of state regulation and protection of infant industries. Similarly, countries in North and East Asia were able to gain the benefits of international trade by avoiding overly-rapid liberalisation.[36] Developing countries must be given the means and support to control the pace and sequencing of reforms. They should also create social and economic safety nets to protect vulnerable groups who may suffer some of the negative consequences of liberalisation.

141. A second major problem concerns market access. While developing countries, under heavy pressure, have removed many of their trade barriers, developed countries have not reciprocated in key areas. In precisely those sectors where developing countries have a comparative advantage, such as agriculture and textiles, the developed countries have protected themselves through both tariff and non-tariff barriers (including rules of origin, standards and technical barriers) and through extensive systems of domestic subsidies, resulting in dumped exports. The European Union's Common Agricultural Policy is one of the most notorious culprits.[37] Each cow in the EU is subsidised $2.20 per day, while around 40 per cent of the world's population lives on less that $2 per day.[38] The recent increase in US farm subsidies has

exacerbated the situation. The World Bank estimates that the costs for developing countries of protectionism in the developed world amount to $100 billion each year.

142. The Fancourt Commonwealth Declaration of 1999 stresses that greater equity in global markets requires addressing the trade privileges of developed countries. Developed countries, including those in the Commonwealth, should be encouraged to accelerate liberalisation of their own economies to increase market access for developing countries. Small states within the Commonwealth feel particularly vulnerable to the inequalities of the global trading system, and need support in order to diversify exports and adjust to the erosion of trade preferences.

143. Third, developing countries lack influence in the decision-making processes that create the rules and regulations of the international trade regime, particularly in the World Trade Organisation (WTO). Despite the WTO being based on 'one country – one vote', in practice decision-making occurs through informal channels that lack accountability and transparency, and it is dominated by the wealthy industrialised countries.[39] Lack of technical capacity and financial resources limits the influence of most poor countries in WTO negotiations. A more democratic international trade system would build on the breakthrough in Seattle to promote reforms to the WTO that would permit greater input and participation from developing countries. Similarly, challenging the secretive nature of WTO decision-making would promote accountability and transparency. Finally, expanding technical support to developing Commonwealth countries would be a means of increasing their capacity to negotiate and implement their obligations within the WTO in ways that are consistent with their development interests. A recent set of proposals to reform the WTO is discussed in Box 4.

144. A final problematic aspect of the international trade system is that the existing rules are not sufficiently oriented towards pro-poor development. The breakdown of talks in the Cancun WTO ministerial meeting in 2003 was extremely disappointing. It is crucial that all countries commit to a positive outcome of the Doha Development Round. This requires all parties to reaffirm commitment to a transparent, rules-based multilateral trading system and to avoid recourse to fortress-building regional or bi-lateral arrangements. They must continue making efforts to reduce trade-distorting subsidies and other barriers to trade, particularly in agriculture. It is clear that there is a need for co-operation and flexibility to deliver the Doha Development Agenda.

145. Cancun demonstrated that developing countries have never been better organised. The industrialised countries should recognise this new reality: that developing countries are no longer prepared to operate separately in trade negotiations. 'Business as usual' is likely to generate frustration that could lead to a crisis of confidence in the WTO. This would be in the interests of neither the developed nor the developing

world. The rules and decision-making systems of the WTO should be reformed to enable developing countries to pursue their development objectives.

Private flows

146. The private sector is the engine of growth in output, employment and incomes in contemporary economies. The economic diversification and wealth creation necessary for sustained growth and development, a *sine qua non* for poverty reduction, cannot take place without an expansion of competitive private sector capacity. The development of a business-friendly environment that promotes pro-poor growth is a matter of the highest priority. It is essential to encourage both high quality foreign direct investment (FDI) and domestic investment to create stable employment, expand domestic demand and transfer new technologies from the developed to the developing world.[40]

Box 4: Democratising the WTO system and Addressing Key Development Issues

An innovative proposal to help make democracy work for a pro-poor international trade regime is the set of holistic reforms to the WTO system suggested by Third World Network (TWN) as part of UNDP's 'Trade and Sustainable Human Development' project.* The proposals cover areas including:

• **Textiles and agriculture**
Developed countries should comply with their obligations under the Uruguay Round to phase out their textile and garment quotas by 2005 and should be encouraged to accelerate liberalisation. In agriculture, domestic and export subsidies and tariff peaks in developed countries should be drastically reduced.

• **Intellectual property rights**
Among the measures necessary to make TRIPS more balanced is to agree that all living organisms and their parts, and all living processes, cannot be patented. In addition, while patents have obvious importance in encouraging research and development, nothing in the TRIPS Agreement should prevent members from taking measures that can make medicines accessible and affordable to the public at times of health crises.

• **Services**
The liberalisation of services under the General Agreement on Trade in Services (GATS) is mainly benefiting developed countries as they tend to have service enterprises with a greater capacity than those in developing countries. In addition, the lack of data on the services trade means that it is difficult to assess the impact of GATS on developing countries. Until the problem of lack of data is

147. At present many of the potential benefits of private investment flows for pro-poor development are being lost. For instance, while FDI flows to developing countries have been increasing, a large proportion of profits continue to be repatriated to the North. For every $1 entering a developing country as FDI, 30 cents leaves the country. In sub-Saharan Africa profit repatriation is three-quarters of FDI, which reflects a high dependence on extractive industries.[41]

148. Companies increasingly realise that they have responsibilities that accompany their rights. These responsibilities are seen to include upholding human rights, particularly economic and social rights relating to labour, in addition to meeting national and international environmental standards.[42] Consequently many large corporations have introduced voluntary codes of conduct and 'Triple Bottom Line Accounting' that provides information on their social and environmental contributions as well as their financial profitability in their annual reports. Some firms are

---

tackled, developing countries should not be expected to undertake further obligations. Developed countries should take concrete steps (e.g., provide incentives to domestic firms) to encourage imports of services from developing countries, and measures should be taken to better facilitate the temporary movement of labour from developing to developed countries.

• **Improve the basic structure**
Developing countries and civil society should be given more voice in decision-making within the WTO. There should be formal acceptance that developing countries undertake lower levels of obligation than developed countries, and thus not have their special treatment limited to longer implementation periods, as is currently the case in practice. It should be recognised that developing countries need the flexibility to raise and reduce tariffs to help support the growth of specific sectors, particularly infant industries and the technology sector.

The proposed reforms are noteworthy not only for their comprehensive and integrated approach to creating a pro-poor trade regime, but also for their democratic content. They promote greater equality between the North and the South, improve accountability and encourage greater developing country participation and representation in decision-making processes. This set of reforms is not a blueprint endorsed by the Expert Group for the Doha Round of Multilateral Trade Negotiations but rather constitutes one of a number of possible innovative ways of making democracy work for pro-poor development.

* *Third World Network 2001, 6-16, 79-91. For alternative sets of proposals see, for example, Oxfam 2002a, 250-258 and UNDP 2002, 121.*

attempting to implement internationally agreed codes of conduct, such as the Organisation for Economic Co-operation and Development (OECD) Principles of Corporate Governance and Guidelines for Multinational Enterprises, and the Commonwealth Business Council's 16 Point Programme for Investment.[43]

149. While self-regulation through codes of conduct has been successful in some instances, in other cases it has not. For example, a number of major companies have codes of conduct that do not mention the right of a worker to join a trade union or engage in collective bargaining – core labour standards set out by the International Labour Organisation (ILO). Although voluntary codes are an important step in encouraging companies to respect basic rights, there is no substitute for government enforcement of these rights when they are already enshrined in international law or good practice, or the laws of the company's own home country (see Box 5).

150. Better monitoring and more effective prosecution of corporate bribery are essential for accountability and transparency.[44] The Chairman of Transparency International recently highlighted the 'criminal bribe-paying activities' of transnational corporations headquartered in industrial countries.[45] Additionally, reforming political party financing so that private sector contributions and other influences do not unduly distort the democratic process is a method of challenging corruption.[46]

151. Companies could also take greater individual initiative to use democracy as a means of promoting pro-poor development. For instance, in industries such as mining that use the natural resources of an isolated area, firms or national governments could arrange to provide equity or royalties to local communities, consult the representatives of local communities and supply employment and community services such as health, training and education. More generally, companies can promote participation by making their employees more integrated stakeholders, such as through extending employee share ownership schemes (ESOPS) throughout the firm.[47] Such approaches, which could be encouraged in both transnational and domestic firms, are an effective means of promoting democratic values such as participation and representation.[48] Greater participation of poor communities in business could also occur through governments making more effort to promote small businesses, such as by backing micro-credit schemes or reducing the costs of business registration.[49] Opportunities should also be taken to promote women's entrepreneurship, which has had an important impact on development in Commonwealth and other countries.[50]

152. While improving the general business environment is a significant means of promoting pro-poor development, it is also important to consider specific issues related to the stability of private capital flows. During the 1990s private capital flows became the main source of external financing for developing countries, while official financing became relatively less important.[51] The Monterrey Consensus, adopted by

Box 5: Creating a Business Environment for Pro-poor Development

Developing countries, like all economies, require a business environment that encourages investment. Potential investors look to sovereign risk and a satisfactory return on their investment as key components of their investment criteria. Those countries with a stable democratic government, transparent administrative processes and a fair and effective legal system have proven to attract the majority of the investment that is necessary to promote pro-poor development.

The Commonwealth and the international community are concerned with corporate behaviour and responsibility throughout all Commonwealth countries, but particularly in developing countries. The Expert Group supports a self-regulatory approach to ensuring corporate good governance and social responsibility.

The Group encourages governments within the Commonwealth to ensure, either through legislation or practical measures, that all companies operating within their jurisdiction abide by the laws of the country from which they originated. In addition, industry groups within a country should be encouraged to work with that country's government to ensure that they self-regulate and monitor their industries. This will ensure that the same standards apply across that industry within the country and therefore help guarantee that the standards are the world's best practice.

The Expert Group believes that there is an important role that the Commonwealth could play should the Commonwealth Heads of Government so determine. This would be to provide experts from within the wealthier industrial countries' public services to conduct random audits within those Commonwealth countries that would like such assistance. This would result in the development, over time, of a 'Commonwealth yard-stick'. In addition, the Group encourages all Commonwealth countries to enact legislation to ensure that companies based in their country, when acting internationally, comply with their country's own legislative standards.

Commonwealth countries should also ensure that their financial institutions lending to businesses operating in other countries comply with the laws of the countries in which they originated. This is essential if one reflects on the environmental tragedies that have occurred among the smaller or emerging countries: These have, in the vast majority of instances, been financed by major banks that could have ensured compliance.

Heads of Government at the UN Financing for Development Conference in Monterrey in March 2002, stresses that private international capital flows, particularly FDI, along with international financial stability, are vital complements to national and international development efforts. It is essential, according to the Monterrey Consensus, to facilitate direct private investment flows to developing countries, least developed countries (particularly in Africa) and small island developing states.[52] Similarly, Commonwealth Finance Ministers, in their meeting in London in May 2002, stressed the importance of securing stronger and more stable flows of private finance to developing countries. This is also discussed in the Commonwealth Code of Good Practice for Promoting Private Flows and Coping with Capital Market Volatility.[53]

153. The globalisation of capital markets has resulted in highly volatile and speculative capital flows that are damaging developing countries. Economic crises in these countries have taken a variety of forms, such as the closure of businesses, huge increases in unemployment, cuts in spending on social welfare programmes and substantial rises in income poverty and wealth inequality. Unregulated international capital flows are increasingly considered to resemble the activities of a casino.[54] In addition, many small states are especially disadvantaged in international capital markets, and find it difficult to access private capital and protect themselves from unstable capital flows.[55]

154. It is clear that more effective regulation of international capital markets is required to promote development in poor countries. The IMF itself has recently concluded that the rapid liberalisation of the capital account appears to have been accompanied, in some cases, by increased vulnerability to crises. It now advocates that financial integration with the global economy should be approached cautiously, with strong domestic financial institutions and stable macroeconomic frameworks. There should, therefore, be a case-by-case approach to the pace and sequencing of capital account liberalisation, taking into account specific national circumstances.

155. The liberalisation of capital markets has also facilitated international money laundering and the financing of terrorism. Money laundering is often the result of organised looting by governments of public funds. The effects of money laundering and the efforts to combat it have had a particular impact on small states in the Commonwealth.[56] The Commonwealth Secretariat has been assisting countries to implement the 40 recommendations of the Financial Action Task Force on Money Laundering (FATF) and the provisions of Security Council Resolution 1373.[57] Implementation of these recommendations is essential for promoting accountability and transparency, and for safeguarding vulnerable financial systems against abuse.

Debt

156. Over the past three decades the external debt of developing countries has increased around forty-fold in monetary terms. Debt servicing has grown at an even greater rate: The debt service of low-income countries now greatly exceeds new inflows, leaving net transfers in 2000 at negative $29bn.[58] Many developing countries have found that their potential resources for pro-poor development are being diverted to repay their international creditors, whether it be with respect to bilateral, multilateral or private sector debt. Only a minority of developing countries have maintained their external debt at sustainable levels. Debt crises in developing countries can have significant contagion effects that threaten global financial stability. As the Commonwealth Fancourt Declaration emphasises, there is an urgent need to tackle the unsustainable debt burdens of developing countries.

157. The heavily indebted poor countries (HIPC) initiative, launched in 1996 and enhanced in 1999, was designed to confront the problem of multilateral, bilateral and commercial debt in some of the world's poorest states. Official debt alone totals around $150bn (in 1999 nominal terms).[59] The initiative has had important positive effects, particularly on recipient countries' ability and willingness to increase domestic spending on education and HIV/AIDS programmes, and has improved - budget management more generally.[60] HIPC debt relief enabled Uganda to achieve universal primary education. Private investors are also gaining confidence about directing their funds towards countries participating in the HIPC Initiative. For the 26 countries benefiting from HIPC relief, debt service payments are projected to be cut in half over the next two decades.

158. Although bringing some relief, the HIPC initiative has been criticised on a number of grounds. First, the average annual reduction (from 1999 to 2002) in debt service in HIPCs has been only around $1.3bn.[61] In addition, not all creditors have agreed to reduce their HIPC debts. It is also a matter of concern that an increasing number of HIPCs continue to face litigation on their commercial debt. The initiative has also not proved to be sufficiently flexible to cope with the effects of exogenous shocks. Furthermore, due to low commodity export prices and weak growth rates, debtor countries are less easily able to achieve the performance track record required to reach the 'completion point' – that point at which creditors are satisfied that sufficient measures have been taken by a country to make debt repayment sustainable, if there is some relief. (The debt sustainability ratios are the net present value of debt to exports of 150 per cent and, in exceptional cases, net present value of debt to fiscal revenue of 250 per cent.) Another criticism is that when HIPC relief is financed from stagnant or declining official development assistance (ODA) budgets of donor countries, it simply serves to divert resources from moderately indebted to severely indebted countries, and thus may not add significantly to total development

Box 6: Delivering on Debt Relief through the HIPC Initiative

In a recent paper written for the Commonwealth Secretariat, Nancy Birdsall and Brian Deese outline proposals for improving the enhanced HIPC initiative. Among their proposals are the following:*

• **Deepening debt relief**
Heavily indebted poor countries need more resources to help tackle poverty, especially in the areas of education, health and infrastructure. This is particularly the case in small African countries that are highly dependent on primary commodity production and exports, and are affected by the HIV/AIDS crisis. Debt repayments in HIPCs should be limited to a ceiling of 2 per cent of GNP. This ceiling is not only sustainable, but also prevents debt service from unduly sapping resources from development programmes. The approach would relieve $700 million of debt service for 2003 in the eleven HIPCs that are not yet at the 2 per cent debt service to GNP ratio.

• **Insuring HIPCs against external shocks**
A major problem faced by HIPCs is that their debt repayments are hampered by exogenous shocks such as poor weather or falls in export prices. An IMF study showed that around half the HIPCs receiving debt relief would again be in an unsustainable debt situation by 2003, and that in most cases this was due to lower than predicted export growth caused by the global economic slowdown and the fall in international commodity prices. Uganda, the first country to achieve 'completion point', has seen its debt rise above the sustainability threshold due to depressed coffee prices. Even so, the estimates for debt repayments have been based on overly optimistic predictions of future economic and export growth. HIPC vulnerability to external shocks could be addressed if such countries were granted additional debt relief when shocks that eroded debt sustainability were shown to be beyond their control. This issue is already partly addressed in the existing HIPC framework, in which it is possible for countries to obtain extra debt relief for a limited period in 'exceptional' circumstances.

This 'topping up' option, however, lacks predictability in its application and is available for too short a time period. A more predictable and sustainable insurance facility is required to confront the problems of the HIPC initiative. In order to help reassure investors that a country's debt burden is sustainable, the facility should be available for ten years. Each year the IMF would calculate whether the 2 per cent debt repayment/GNP ratio described above was being exceeded; if so, the IMF could then assess the proportion of the excess attributable to ex-ogenous shocks, and further debt relief could be granted accordingly. This process would be open to public scrutiny. Costing an estimated $500bn over ten years, the insurance facility could be financed from IMF gold reserves, which have ceased

> to play any serious monetary function.
>
> These reforms to the HIPC initiative would, like the policies suggested in the sections above, serve a dual purpose. On the one hand they could help contribute to development in countries with high debt burdens, as debt repayments draw government funds away from poverty alleviation programmes and can aggravate financial instability. But such reforms would also be consistent with democratic values. Making debt relief more contingent upon the particular problems facing debtor countries, such as weak commodity prices, low growth or HIV/AIDS, is a way of giving states a greater chance of responding to their citizens' needs.
>
> * *Birdsall and Deese 2002, para. 20-41. The proposals draw on their book* Delivering on Debt Relief. *Alternative proposals for debt relief appear in Akyüz 2002, 12-15, Global Financial Governance Initiative 2002 and Dodhia 2002, para. 32.*

assistance. Finally, the new poverty reduction strategy papers (PRSPs) announced in 1999, in which governments (aided by the IMF and World Bank) undertake consultations with civil society to develop country-owned poverty reduction strategies that would form the basis for the HIPC initiative and other donor assistance, have been subject to criticism, including that there has been a lack of effective participation by local poor communities (see below).

159. Because of these various problems a major challenge is to find a way of making the HIPC initiative more generous, flexible and sensitive to local needs, and allowing for relief to be more rapidly triggered.[62] Some proposals for doing so are discussed in Box 6. There must also be a commitment to gender-sensitive decision-making in the improvement of the initiative. It should be recognised that long-term debt sustainability can only be attained by reducing the risks associated with these economies and increasing their resilience through diversification. In addition the Expert Group underscores the importance of all multilateral creditors moving, as a minimum, to 40 per cent grant financing in line with IDA 13 (the 13th Replenishment of the World Bank's International Development Association) for vulnerable HIPCs. In addition, the OECD Development Assistance Committee (DAC) bilateral donors that have not done so should provide 100 per cent grant financing to these countries. Furthermore, the quest for more flexible procedures should continue to enable conflict-affected countries to reach the 'decision point' – the point when a country's interim report is approved and it qualifies for debt relief under the initiative. Debt relief must be designed to be sensitive to the problems of particular developing countries, such as low commodity export prices, natural disasters, public health crises or lack of economic diversification and weak growth, as means of promoting pro-poor development.

160. Creating international procedures so that developing countries could resort to a debt standstill in a crisis situation, and subsequently seek approval for their actions from an international body, could be an effective method of supporting development while also creating international mechanisms of accountability, thereby helping make democracy work for pro-poor development.[63]

Aid

161. ODA is needed to supplement improved trading opportunities, debt relief and private flows to help poor countries out of the poverty trap and into sustained development. International aid gives developing countries, particularly the most impoverished least developed countries (LDCs), an opportunity to build up their physical and human resource bases, and subsequently to shift from aid dependence. It also enables them to strengthen institutions, reduce transaction costs and enhance the capacity for a supply-side response in their economies. Small states within the Commonwealth have encouraged donors to increase aid flows to help with their transition to coping with the global economy. While some analysts question the effectiveness of aid, the available evidence clearly shows how aid can increase aggregate savings, investment and growth, and contribute to long-term poverty reduction more generally.[64] Aid can also help stabilise countries affected by events such as conflicts, earthquakes or famines. There are, however, two major problems with existing aid arrangements: Absolute levels of aid are too low and aid is not sufficiently effective.

162. Current ODA is around $56bn a year. But to meet the MDGs, calculations by the UN and others suggest that an additional $40-70bn is required. This means roughly doubling the amount of aid to 0.5 per cent of GNP in industrialised countries.[65] Most countries give far below this level (the USA grants around 0.1 per cent) and only five countries (Denmark, Luxembourg, the Netherlands, Norway and Sweden) provide above 0.7 per cent of GNP, the target agreed upon at the UN in 1970.[66] Moreover, despite the continuing prevalence of global poverty, wealthy countries are effectively giving less international aid than in the past. In real per capita terms, net ODA disbursements to LDCs dropped 46 per cent between 1990 and 2000.[67] These falls have been occurring even in countries considered to have good policy environments. In addition, a considerable amount of aid promised to LDCs never arrives.[68]

163. In response to the shortfall of ODA, the UK Treasury recently called for the creation of an International Finance Facility (IFF) that would constitute a commitment by donor countries to substantially increase resources for developing countries to meet the MDGs by 2015. The facility would raise funds on international capital markets and distribute them in the form of grants and concessional loans.[69] The principle of securitising future aid flows is not inconsistent with the approach adopted to finance large infrastructure projects or raise funding from capital markets for the

Table 3: 'Going it alone, with strings attached'*

All aid is not the same. Some countries give a large share of their aid in the form of technical co-operation (TC), which is rarely demand driven and is often largely spent on well-paid advisers from rich countries. Some of the remaining aid is often 'tied' to the purchase of the donor country's products, meaning that the recipient cannot use aid to buy from other countries that make those things more cheaply. Countries also vary in how much of their aid goes to support collective international aid institutions and how much goes only through their own bilateral aid agencies – often without significant co-ordination with other donors.

	Share of all aid spending on donor-country goods or services (%)a	Share of all aid given bilaterally (%)b
Australia	80	74
Austria	54	65
Belgium	54	57
Canada	79	69
Denmark	19	59
Finland	46	58
France	64	73
Germany	61	59
Greece	87	41
Ireland	6	61
Italy	93	25
Japan	37	68
Netherlands	37	69
New Zealand	53	79
Norway	17	73
Portugal	84	75
Spain	46	61
Sweden	11	70
Switzerland	21	74
United Kingdom	43	66
United States	91	75
AVERAGE	**54**	**64**

Note: All data on tied aid and all data on TC and bilateral aid are from each country's 2001 report to OECD on its percentage of tied aid, except for Austria (2000 report to OECD), New Zealand (1992) and the United States (1996).
a This is the sum of two numbers. The first is the share of gross aid commitments that is given as TC. The second is the share of all non-TC gross aid commitments that is 'tied'. A small amount of aid is classified as 'partially untied'; half of this amount is included in the tied share. b Calculated as 1 minus the ratio of 'contributions to multilateral institutions' to 'total official development assistance'.

Source: OECD Development Assistance Committee, DAC Online Database, http://www.oecd.org/htm/M00005000/M00005347.htm#dac/o

* *This table, including both the data and text, is a full reproduction of Figure 1 in Birdsall and Clemens 2003, 4.*

World Bank and regional development banks. The fact that the IFF would have no immediate impact on budgets is particularly attractive at a time when major donors are currently experiencing budgetary constraints. If a wider group of governments fails to endorse a new facility, Commonwealth governments could adapt the structure of the IFF to mobilise resources within the Commonwealth.

164. The reasons for the ineffectiveness of much aid are complex. Part of the problem concerns the lack of co-ordination among donors. Countries are faced, for example, with multiple standards and reporting requirements, which can result in administrative inefficiency and wasted resources. Donors have also shown themselves to be inflexible, often tying aid to procurement or requiring countries to meet stringent and frequently inappropriate conditions for aid disbursement. Global earmarked funds have in some ways eroded the decision-making authority of national governments. In addition, too much aid has been diverted to finance debt service rather than channelled into development purposes.[70]

165. Some of the problems of the current international aid regime are depicted in Table 3, taken from a recent paper published by the Centre for Global Development. It shows how a large proportion of aid is tied to the purchase of donor countries' goods and services, and how a significant share of aid is given bilaterally rather than through collective and co-ordinated international efforts. The data suggest that developed countries may be failing to meet MDG 8 – 'to develop a global partnership for development', including through more generous ODA for countries committed to poverty reduction. Further data on compliance with MDG 8 among developed Commonwealth countries appear in Appendix A.

166. A related problem is the lack of co-ordination between donors and government anti-poverty strategies. The introduction of PRSPs in 1999 was partly intended to deal with this difficulty. Low-income countries would prepare their own national poverty reduction strategies (with advice from the IMF and World Bank and in consultation with civil society), and if deemed satisfactory by the Fund and the Bank, the PRSPs would provide the basis for concessional assistance and debt relief from the Fund, the Bank and the international donor community as a whole. The PRSP process, while still at an early stage of its development, appears to have encouraged dialogue between donors, governments and civil society, and is having some beneficial effects on budgetary processes.[71]

167. The PRSPs have, however, been subject to criticism. While the process of policy formulation has changed in some ways, the content of policies has not; PRSPs often seem to reinforce policy directions already in place. Even when PRSPs are 'country owned', they are frequently incompatible with the conditionality attached to HIPC decision and completion point documents, Poverty Reduction and Growth

Facility (PRGF) arrangements or Poverty Reduction Support Credits (PRSC). Civil society associations, and sometimes even parliaments, feel marginalised from the PRSP process, and the PRSPs also tend to neglect the impact of trade liberalisation policies on poverty, and to be insensitive to gender issues. While the IMF and World Bank acknowledge some of these problems, few criticisms, as yet, have been addressed sufficiently in reappraisals and adjustments of the system.[72] The PRSP process is expected to be continuous and iterative; as such, it provides the scope to address these issues, as long as governments are committed to the process and donors are willing to align themselves behind beneficiary priorities.

168. Countries with 'endowed handicaps' based on smallness, remoteness or being landlocked experience particularly difficult challenges in attracting investment. Priority needs to be attached to identifying innovative market-friendly instruments for sharing risk through the use of official resources to assist them to compensate for their endowed handicaps. Historically, these countries were able to attract investment to develop competitive capacity through the benefits provided by trade preferences, which are now being eroded. The UK Department for International Development's Emerging Africa Infrastructure Fund is an example of such an instrument.

169. Private voluntary flows and aid from non-governmental organisations (NGOs) amount to some $7bn per year (over half of which comes from government sources), which is around 8 per cent of ODA.[73] While NGO aid is generally more effective than official assistance at reaching the poor, such aid does not come without problems. Northern NGOs often operate without sufficient participation from the communities they are intending to benefit. Furthermore, the activities of many NGOs are largely unmonitored by the public or governments, resulting in a lack of accountability and transparency.[74]

170. Democratically-oriented policies can be used to confront the development challenges posed by the international aid regime. National poverty reduction strategies could have more meaningful participation from poor communities and incorporate more comprehensive public information campaigns.[75] Reducing the amount of tied aid that promotes donor commercial interest – often at the expense of national priorities – and reducing excessive conditionality in official assistance as well as providing increased direct budgetary support where appropriate, would give governments greater ownership and control of their own policies. Similarly, greater co-ordination and harmonisation between donors and governments would be a way that donors could show their respect for the sovereignty of developing countries. The good practice papers promoted by the OECD-DAC might provide a model in this area.[76] Priority should be attached to implementing the outcomes of the High Level Forum on Harmonisation (Rome, 24-25 February 2003). An example of how governments and donors can work together more effectively is highlighted in Box 7.

171. For their part, beneficiary countries need to strengthen the accountability and transparency of government revenue and expenditure. Promoting good governance and combating corruption can improve aid effectiveness (see Section 4.3).

172. The Expert Group emphasises that the Commonwealth has a great opportunity to give a lead to the international community to ensure that resources for development are allocated and targeted in accordance with the recipient country's own development programmes and frameworks. Failure in this regard will not only undermine the long-term prospects for economic success but will also undermine democratic processes.

5.2 International Institutions

173. The institutions of global governance, such as the IMF, the World Bank, the WTO and the United Nations and its specialised agencies, all play important roles in facilitating development, alleviating poverty and securing the peace. The Expert Group believes that it is essential to ensure that international institutions pursue these goals in ways that reinforce and strengthen democratic decision-making and democratic culture both within countries and within the institutions themselves.

174. Much policy debate about the institutions of global economic governance centres on making the IMF and World Bank more accountable through tackling their democratic deficits. What is the nature of these democratic deficits? The main problem is one of representation. Nearly half the voting power in the World Bank (46%) and IMF (48%) is held by just seven countries: China, France, Japan, the Russian Federation, Saudi Arabia, the United Kingdom and the United States. Due to a special majority of 85 per cent being required for significant decisions, the United States is effectively able to exercise a veto. Discretionary control over additional resources furthers US influence in both organisations. In contrast, developing countries – the main borrowers – have comparatively little representation. Although they receive 'basic votes', the share of these in voting power has declined from 12.4 to 2.1 per cent.[77] Informal practices are also important. The United States and Europe effectively choose the heads of the World Bank and the IMF respectively. Despite recent reform initiatives, both organisations have also been criticised for their lack of accountability and transparency in decision-making processes, in addition to the limited number of women among top executives. A set of proposals suggested by UNDP to challenge the democratic deficits in the IMF and World Bank is discussed in Box 8.

175. The democratic deficits in the IMF and World Bank have often had detrimental consequences for development. The Bretton Woods Institutions have promoted policy blueprints that are inappropriate for complex economic and political

Box 7: Improving Donor-Government Co-ordination in Tanzania

Tanzania provides a good example of improving donor-government co-ordination as a means of making aid more effective. A recent OECD-DAC country study of Tanzania analyses the greater trust and harmonisation between donors and the government since the mid-1990s. It highlights the following:*

• The annual Public Expenditure Reviews (PER) and preparation of the Medium Term Expenditure Framework (MTEF)
Introduced by the World Bank in 1996, the PER is now an annual government-led process with wide participation from key sector ministries, most donors and some NGOs and academic institutions.

• The Local Government Reform Programme Basket Fund
In 1997 donors and the government established the Common Basket Fund (CBF), a joint funding mechanism to finance the implementation of the Local Government Reform Programme. The CBF is overseen by a committee comprising donor and government representatives, and is mandated to approve annual work programmes, authorise budgets, release funds into the basket and review external audit reports.

• Harmonisation around the Tanzania Assistance Strategy (TAS)
In 2002 the government issued the TAS as a 'home-grown' initiative providing a framework for managing foreign aid resources. In the TAS the Government has incorporated many donor concerns, such as promoting good governance, transparency and accountability. The OECD-DAC group of donors have established a Harmonisation Sub-Group to generate responses from donors to the TAS. A process has been established to reach a consensus between donors and the Government on managing aid.

Despite some difficulties, the process of harmonisation between donors and the Government of Tanzania has met with much success. Greater co-ordination is enabling aid to be more effective in assisting with the implementation of the PRSP. There is still a need, however, to bring some donors more closely into the harmonisation initiatives. The improved co-ordination also has important democratic elements. Ownership of aid management is shifting from donors to the Government. Harmonisation processes have included considerable participation from different sectors, including NGOs. Some policy programmes that involve greater donor-government co-ordination, such as that concerning local government reform, support democratic values such as local democracy. More effective monitoring of the donor-government relationship has also contributed to greater transparency of international aid flows and programmes.

* Ronsholt 2002. See also UNCTAD 2002, 196.

> **Box 8: Challenging the Democratic Deficit in Global Financial Institutions**
>
> UNDP's *Human Development Report 2002* is one of many studies that highlights a possible reform package that could increase developing country representation in the IMF and World Bank, and help tackle the problem of the democratic deficit in these institutions.* The first proposal is to increase the proportion of basic votes of developing countries relative to the voting power of developed countries, so that the developed countries can no longer be so dominant. The second main proposal is to enhance the voice of developing countries, and to increase both accountability and transparency, by having an open selection procedure for electing the heads of the two institutions. Additionally, the number of seats allocated to developing countries on the executive boards should be increased, as should the number of women in top positions. Third, there could be greater efforts to make the institutions more accountable for their actions, such as through: (1) publishing the minutes of executive board meetings; (2) improving follow up of independent evaluations, including those of the World Bank's Operations Evaluation Department and the IMF's Office of Independent Evaluation; and (3) enhancing the ability of poor communities affected by decisions and projects in developing countries to access dispute mechanisms, such as the World Bank's Inspection Panel.
>
> The policies outlined above, although not blueprints endorsed by the Expert Group, are possible ways of promoting pro-poor development and tackling the democratic deficit in the IMF and World Bank. Greater representation of developing countries, more effective methods of participation and increased accountability and transparency are good for democracy and also a means of generating policies that are more sensitive to the needs of disadvantaged populations facing poverty in developing countries.
>
> * *UNDP 2002, 112-122. For other proposals see Global Financial Governance Initiative 2002 and Akyüz 2002, 15-25. Some of the following proposals are discussed in International Monetary Fund and World Bank 2003.*

realities in developing countries. IMF adjustment policies, including high interest rates, currency depreciation and large budgetary cuts, have often been associated with poverty and inequality increases. According to many scholars IMF-supported measures such as full capital account convertibility contributed to substantial economic instability in East Asia and the Russian Federation. World Bank projects have often occurred without sufficient consultation with local populations and have had negative development consequences.[78]

176. The recent trend towards a greater focus on poverty reduction in reform programmes supported by the IMF and World Bank is to be welcomed, as is the effort to enhance developing country 'voice' in the international financial institutions. The World Bank now uses environmental impact assessments, social impact assessments and other measures in an effort to make its projects more sensitive to local populations. Reforms including greater disclosure of information by the Bretton Woods Institutions, the PRSP process, the IMF's creation of regional technical assistance centres and the Bank's decentralisation of its country offices, have contributed to developing country voice and capacity-building, and created greater transparency. Current proposals to increase the voice of developing countries include providing developing country chairs with greater technical and research support and increasing the number of executive directors.[79] The good intentions of the international financial institutions must be translated into concrete practices.

177. The WTO's decision-making system is nominally democratic in that it is based on 'one country – one vote'. In practice, it needs to be reformed so that developing country members can participate more effectively, especially in the drafting of negotiating texts. The WTO needs to become an organisation that truly respects the interests of developing countries.

178. There is a need to encourage deeper participation of poor communities in the PRSP process, and to monitor the extent to which other policies and programmes in the IMF, World Bank and WTO might be bypassing or inadvertently eroding democratic processes and institutions at the national and sub-national levels. It is also important to ensure that international economic and political institutions are themselves models of good practice in respect of democratic accountability, transparency and participation. In these ways, democracy can work for pro-poor development.

5.3 Peace and Security

179. The Fancourt Commonwealth Declaration of 1999 recognises the fragility of global peace and security. One of the most distinguishing features of the post-Cold War period is the rise of intra-state conflict. Between 1990 and 2001 there were 57 major armed conflicts in 45 different locations, and all but three of these conflicts were internal.[80] Many of the conflicts have spilled over into bordering countries, resulting in regional instability. In some cases neighbouring countries have intervened in civil conflicts to fuel tensions, usually for ethnic or extractive purposes. In addition, civil conflicts have not only caused the massive internal displacement of millions of people, but have contributed to the international refugee crisis that has affected countries in both the South and North. Internal conflicts have sometimes led to the phenomenon of failed states, in which central government authority collapses, as has occurred in Afghanistan and Somalia. A large proportion of civil conflicts have

occurred in fragile new democracies in developing countries.[81] As part of the global effort to ensure peace and security, the Commonwealth Secretary-General's good offices have been increasingly invoked in conflict resolution.[82]

180. But global peace and security have also been threatened by other problems. One of these is terrorism. Since 11 September 2001, governments across the globe have stepped up their efforts to confront terrorist groups. In October 2001, Commonwealth Heads of Government condemned terrorism and "any nation which harbours, supports or provides assistance to terrorist activity".[83]

181. Terrorism has also become enmeshed with other existing problems such as drug trafficking, the arms trade and money laundering. The rise of organised crime – both transnational and domestic – and terrorism have altered the very nature of crime and created distinct challenges for governments across the globe. Crime can no longer be addressed as a local matter. Most serious crime has transnational components and effects and requires a co-operative effort to respond to it. Increasingly by its nature, complexity and wide-ranging impact, such crime constitutes a direct threat to social and political stability. Organised crime and terrorism are limiting the development opportunities of poor countries in a number of ways, for example by diverting scarce resources to fight crime, deterring investment, and through funds being siphoned out of the legitimate economy. A related problem concerns citizen security linked to common crime. In both the North and South there has been an enormous increase in violent crime in recent decades, often committed by mafias, bandits and gangs. Survey data shows how fear of crime is frequently among citizens' greatest daily concerns.[84]

182. Finally, the proliferation of small arms is a key problem for peace and security. A recent United Nations Conference on the Illicit Trade in Small Arms and Light Weapons in All its Aspects highlighted the presence of 500 million small arms in the world and that 40 per cent of the trade is illegal.[85]

183. The causes of these peace and security problems are extremely complicated. They include factors related to the extent to which domestic political institutions can resolve potential conflict, national and international economic structures, cultural and social divisions, the changing geopolitical balance, and historical legacies. Conflict usually emerges through a combination of such factors. Among the various causes ethnic and religious intolerance has been at the root of much conflict; and the international arms trade, for which industrialised country governments bear great responsibility, has both encouraged violence and perpetuated the length of many civil conflicts. Former colonial powers also often left countries with antagonisms that are now being resolved through armed conflict. Apart from these factors, it is essential to acknowledge the link between poverty and violence. In the past two decades internal conflicts have not only emerged in countries that suffer from ethnic tension or have

disputes inherited from the age of empire, but in some of the poorest countries of the world, especially in Africa. It is clear that poverty and inequality can contribute to the tensions that lead to civil war, support for fundamentalist groups and common crime.

184. Poverty is also a consequence of conflict and insecurity. Without peace and security farmers cannot grow and harvest crops and businesses do not have an environment in which they can invest. Scarce resources are directed towards fighting wars, obtaining private security or pursuing terrorists. Infrastructure is destroyed, food is difficult to distribute, and internal displacement and refugee exoduses prevent people from effectively engaging in productive activity. Long-term economic planning can become an impossibility.[86] The consequences of conflict can persist long into post-conflict periods. It can take years, for example, for a previously war-torn country to rebuild basic economic infrastructure.

185. Numerous Commonwealth countries have been affected by acute social and ethnic conflict. Conflicts in corners of the world as diverse as Bougainville and Sierra Leone have destroyed health systems, education services and agriculture, and generated a culture of intolerance. Ethnic and social conflicts have occurred in Fiji Islands, Kenya, the Solomon Islands, Sri Lanka and Uganda. Bangladesh, India and Pakistan have suffered from internal and external conflicts. In all these countries, and many others, conflict and insecurity have exacerbated poverty.[87] In several new democracies ethnicity and religion have been used by party leaders to promote their political objectives, while secular politics have been eroded. In addition, ethnic tensions have been fuelled by electoral systems that favour some groups over others, and by educational systems and media that fail to promote a culture of tolerance. It is essential, therefore, to recognise the reality of multiculturalism and to support cultural diversity. High priority must be attached to promoting political mobilisation based on inclusive platforms and ideologies.

186. The Expert Group is particularly concerned that the international community is failing to provide timely logistical and financial support in a number of conflict situations, particularly in Africa, where domestic efforts to contain conflict have been made and have failed (Box 9). Without such support regional and sub-regional efforts to address conflict cannot proceed.

187. There are various ways of using democracy to promote peace and security. Some internationally mediated peace processes to end civil wars have attempted to incorporate participation by groups in civil society, providing a democratic grassroots element to conflict resolution. In Sierra Leone, the Commonwealth has been backing a number of initiatives involving women, men and youth that support post-conflict reconstruction and peace building at the national and local levels.[88] Such approaches not only contribute to peace but also uphold and promote democratic values such as

participation, local democracy and gender rights.

188. A recent report emphasises that religious strife, civil wars and ethnic tensions are often due to "the absence or denial of free cultural expression as embodied in cultural diversity".[89] Policies that contribute to greater cultural diversity and religious or ethnic tolerance, such as the incorporation of multi-ethnic and pluricultural themes into educational curricula, can be a means of promoting peace. They can also support civil rights, such as freedom of religion, and group rights including the right of indigenous peoples to establish and control their education systems and institutions in a manner appropriate to their cultural methods of teaching and learning.

189. Reducing arms sales to governments that use weapons to subordinate their civilian populations can help protect human rights, while fighting the illegal arms trade upholds respect for the rule of law. Strengthening judiciaries to challenge abuses committed by the military and police, and ensuring lack of impunity for past human rights violations, also bolsters the rule of law. The rule of law will be further strengthened by more effective legal provisions to fight terrorism and organised crime. At the same time, anti-terrorist policies should maintain respect for civil liberties in order to be consistent with democratic values.[90] Finally, community policing

---

Box 9: Encouraging International Co-operation to Support Peace and Security in Africa

Conflicts not only impoverish the poor but also erode processes of democratisation. They constitute a major obstacle to Africa's renaissance. Recognising this reality African states have been pursing policies aimed at addressing this scourge. In addition to national efforts, sub-regional and continental mechanisms have been established to respond to the crisis situations emanating from conflicts in countries such as Burundi, Democratic Republic of the Congo and Liberia.

Preventing, containing and resolving conflicts are daunting but urgent challenges. They require resources in addition to political will. For these efforts to have a reasonable chance of success they need to be augmented by international support. Such support is particularly needed for peace missions and peacekeeping. Where such support has been forthcoming it has had a decisive impact. Sierra Leone is a case in point. But the reality is that such support is the exception rather than the rule.

There are a number of examples where African states' readiness to act decisively in deploying peace missions or peacekeeping has been frustrated by the lack of requisite means and uncertain or excessively delayed reaction by the international community. Three cases come to mind.

In 1994, in the immediate aftermath of the genocide in Rwanda, the UN was keen to deploy peacekeepers and undertake other peace initiatives. The UN Secretary-General

projects to reduce common crime are a means of democratising security to build peace.[91] These kinds of strategies can help pro-poor development through ensuring peace and security, while simultaneously upholding and promoting democratic values.

190. The military invasion of Iraq has raised discussion about whether it is legitimate and necessary to impose democracy by force. Some commentators have argued that 'regime change' through military action by democratic countries can be an effective means of establishing democracy in undemocratic states. The Expert Group is wary of this approach to democratisation. Such actions may not only have weak foundations in international law, but also divert scarce public funds into military spending, have serious consequences in terms of loss of life, induce refugee crises, cause other forms of social, political and economic instability as well as divert development resources away from the most needy. For these reasons, the Expert Group believes that democratisation is best achieved using a peaceful but activist approach that encourages dialogue among diverse social sectors and supports local citizen participation in seeking solutions to political injustice. The international community should focus its attention on supporting free and fair elections and helping to build and to strengthen other institutions and processes, such as effective public

---

expressed his frustration at the failure to obtain troops that could be immediately deployed. Utilising the occasion of the inauguration of President Mandela in Pretoria, the then Secretary-General of the Organisation of African Unity (OAU) had consultations with several African Heads of State. As a result of these consultations at least ten African states were ready to send troops without delay provided that the logistical support was found. It was almost six months before such support was forthcoming.

Another example is that of Burundi. Despite universal support for a peace agreement and mediation efforts led by President Mandela, the deployment of peacekeepers has been hampered due to logistical problems. Only South Africa has been set to deploy while Ethiopia and Mozambique have been unable to deploy without external financial and logistical support.

Finally, there is the dramatic case of Liberia, where again the readiness of regional actors to send troops has been handicapped by the lack of commensurate logistical and financial support from the international community.

The message is very clear. Increasingly African states have demonstrated a determination and readiness to address the different dimensions of conflict as well as the preparedness to take appropriate measures in support of conflict resolution and the deployment of peace missions and peacekeepers. But this determination is clearly undermined by the lack of logistical and financial support provided by the international community.

security forces and judicial systems, that are necessary for democratic governance.

5.4 Recommended Actions at the International Level

Promoting free and fair trade

191. The existing multilateral trading system impedes both development and democracy. The Doha Development Round provides powerful countries with an opportunity to demonstrate their commitment to inclusive globalisation, attainment of the Millennium Development Goals (MDGs) and global peace and security.

192. Commonwealth governments could play a vital role in ensuring:

(i) that ongoing trade negotiations, after the failure to reach agreement in Cancun, address the asymmetries of the international trade regime discussed in this Report, such as those related to agriculture (including subsidies and dumping), market access for non-agricultural products and special and differential treatment;

(ii) that poor and vulnerable economies in the Commonwealth are permitted to undertake liberalisation in ways and with phasing that minimise transition costs and do not impact harshly upon the poor within those countries; and

(iii) that trade policy reforms promote gender equity.

193. The Group notes that the Commonwealth Secretariat could usefully expand its programmes to provide technical support to developing Commonwealth countries as a means of increasing their capacity to negotiate and implement their obligations within the WTO system in ways that are consistent with their development interests.

194. The Expert Group believes that Commonwealth Trade Ministers Meetings could assist the Commonwealth's diverse membership to understand each other's interests and concerns. It is noteworthy that consensus reached at Finance Ministers Meetings enabled the Commonwealth to play a leading role in promoting debt relief for heavily indebted poor countries. While the Group recognises that trade interests are more contentious, it is of the view that as a microcosm of the world, the Commonwealth is well placed to seek to facilitate consensus on multilateral trade issues through better understanding of different perspectives and interests. In addition, where there is significant convergence on particular trade issues, the Commonwealth should bring the full weight of the association to bear on advancing the agenda.

195. Commonwealth countries, assisted by the Commonwealth Secretariat, could take initiatives towards a more balanced intellectual property rights regime that is more oriented towards the needs of developing countries, including access to medicines and the protection of the interests of local communities. One possible initiative is a programme to follow up on the recommendations of the Independent Commission on Intellectual Property Rights (CIPR) established by the UK government.

196. Commonwealth countries should facilitate the creation of instruments (or streamlining of existing instruments) to help low-income countries overcome the problem of commodity price volatility and external shocks, and address the issue of the secular decline in commodity prices. The adverse effects of commodity price volatility (especially for the affected countries' ability to attain the MDGs) should also be taken into account in debt relief schemes such as the HIPC initiative and in aid programmes.

Financing for development

197. Poor countries need urgent and substantive increases in the quantity and quality of financial resources if they are to achieve pro-poor development and the MDGs. The Group believes that such resources can be made available by the international community through a number of means and in particular:

(i) innovative mechanisms for doubling ODA to $100 billion such as through the UK proposal for an International Finance Facility which, if not taken up by all countries, could be adapted as a Commonwealth mechanism for raising development resources;

(ii) improving aid effectiveness through, *inter alia,* strengthened aid administration in beneficiary countries, reductions in tied aid and an increase in direct budgetary support, and implementation of the Rome Declaration on Harmonisation;

(iii) support for social safety nets to reduce the impact of poverty on the most vulnerable groups, such as women, children, disadvantaged ethnic groups and indigenous peoples;

(iv) more flexible approaches to debt relief that release adequate resources to support domestically formulated and internationally agreed development programmes, particularly in health and education;

(v) support for measures that enhance greater stability of flows of

> private investment to developing countries; and

(vi) international financing initiatives to assist developing countries (particularly the smallest and most vulnerable) in confronting exogenous shocks such as a sharp deterioration in their terms of trade that threaten to derail otherwise robust development programmes. This could take the form of strengthening IMF and World Bank facilities to enable them to provide more timely, more concessional and more adequate assistance in these circumstances.

198. In respect of all these initiatives and strategies, the Group emphasises that the Commonwealth has a great opportunity to give a lead to the international community to ensure that resources for development are allocated and targeted in accordance with the recipient country's own development programmes and frameworks. Failure in this regard will not only undermine the long-term prospects for economic success but will also undermine the democratic processes outlined above.

199. The Expert Group emphasises the central importance of sound management of both domestic and external debt as a pre-condition for sustained growth. It recognises the valuable role being played by the Commonwealth Secretariat Debt Recording and Management System (CS-DRMS) in many countries and calls upon the Commonwealth Secretariat to continue to assist countries to develop their debt management capacity.

200. Commonwealth countries should continue to press for implementation of the HIPC initiative in ways that ensure debt sustainability for recipient countries.

201. Commonwealth countries should support initiatives such as NEPAD that encourage partnership between governments, the international community, the private sector and civil society to deliver aid and to tackle development problems more generally. The Expert Group recognises that the Commonwealth, as a series of networks encompassing governments, the private sector and civil society, has a comparative advantage in this area.

Stable private flows

202. While the Expert Group does not believe that supranational bodies are required to confront problems of volatile and inadequate private capital flows, it encourages Commonwealth countries to support initiatives that permit low-income countries to take measures to protect themselves from volatile private flows, including a cautious approach to capital account liberalisation.

203. The Expert Group recognises the various ways in which international financial markets can have adverse effects on developing countries. There may be a need for greater transparency of international financial markets, more effective regulation of highly leveraged investment funds and derivatives and stricter rules against insider trading. These issues require further analysis before concrete solutions can be recommended. The Group calls upon the Financial Stability Forum and other relevant institutions to take account of the more fragile conditions in emerging markets in seeking solutions to these issues.

204. The Financial Action Task Force on Money Laundering (FATF) recommendations on combating money laundering and the financing of terrorism impose considerable administrative and legislative burdens. The Group welcomes the special efforts made by Commonwealth donors to provide support in this area and requests them to continue to assist capacity-constrained countries.

International institutions

205. International institutions, including the IMF, the World Bank, the WTO and the United Nations and its specialised agencies, are all playing important roles in facilitating development, reducing poverty and securing the peace. The Group's concern is to ensure that international organisations pursue these goals in ways that reinforce and strengthen democratic decision-making and democratic culture within countries. In this regard, Commonwealth governments are urged:

(i) to encourage deeper participation of poor communities and vulnerable groups in the poverty reduction strategy paper (PRSP) processes of the IMF and World Bank, and to monitor the extent to which other policies and programmes of the IMF, World Bank and WTO might be bypassing or otherwise inadvertently eroding democratic processes and institutions at the national and sub-national levels; and

(ii) to ensure that international institutions (such as the IMF, World Bank, WTO and UN institutions such as the Security Council) are themselves models of good practice in respect of democratic accountability, participation and transparency.

206. The Commonwealth should take advantage of the reach its members have into these institutions to develop productive working relationships with them in order to advance the association's values and objectives.

Peace and security

207. Conflict and insecurity extinguish the prospects of both democracy and

development. Furthermore they impact disproportionately on the poorest in any society. Yet international action in the cases of the poorest and most desperate states in conflict is almost always dilatory and inadequate where domestic efforts to contain conflict have been made and have failed. The Group is particularly concerned that where regional and sub-regional organisations are attempting to address conflict situations such as those in Burundi, Democratic Republic of the Congo and Liberia, which impact on Commonwealth countries, the international community is often failing to provide timely logistical and financial support without which the operations cannot proceed. On this issue, Commonwealth Heads of Government can make a difference by actively helping to mobilise critical international support and resources to facilitate the work of sub-regional or regional peace initiatives that are duly authorised by the United Nations Security Council.

208. Commonwealth Heads of Government should commit to strengthening and encouraging mechanisms for regional conflict resolution and peace-building initiatives through the development of common policy strategies that facilitate citizen participation, such as from women and youth.

209. The Expert Group believes that democracy cannot be imposed by force. The use of force has significant costs, including loss of life, the diversion of scarce public funds into military spending, the creation of political divisions and the exacerbation of social and economic instability. Moreover, such actions have weak foundations in international law. The Group calls upon Commonwealth countries to support democratisation processes that promote peaceful forms of political change and local citizen participation in decision-making processes, and that conform with international law. The Expert Group believes that the Commonwealth has a comparative advantage in promoting and supporting a multilateral approach that is based on peer review, engagement and pressure.

210. The Expert Group emphasises that appropriate power-sharing arrangements are essential in multi-ethnic and multicultural societies. Commonwealth countries should commit to introducing citizenship education that promotes cultural diversity, religious and ethnic tolerance, human rights and democratic values in general, particularly among youth. Commonwealth countries should also commit to ensuring that the communications media, political parties, electoral systems and other institutions do not contribute to racial and ethnic hatred and intolerance (see Section 4.3).

6
Conclusion

211. As the Commonwealth enters the twenty-first century, it has an unprecedented opportunity to promote both democracy and pro-poor development not only as goals in their own right but as interdependent objectives. Democracy, as this Report has endeavoured to show, can work for pro-poor development. Concerted efforts at the local, national and international levels have the potential to transform the Fancourt Commonwealth Declaration on Globalisation and People-Centred Development into reality and to help developing countries achieve the Millennium Development Goals (MDGs).

212. The Expert Group believes that Commonwealth countries and institutions are in a strong position to build on their existing achievements and further support democracy and pro-poor development in member states in significant and innovative ways. Urgent action is required to tackle not only the fragility of democracy but also the extremes of poverty and inequality that exist in many Commonwealth states. As has been discussed, the key reforms include:

- committing to democratic institutions and strengthening democratic culture;
- tackling corruption;
- ensuring democratic accountability of government revenue and expenditure;
- promoting free and fair trade;
- mobilising resources to finance development;
- encouraging democratic accountability, participation and transparency in international institutions; and
- guaranteeing peace and security.

213. The Expert Group stresses the value of developing a means of monitoring progress towards implementing the Recommendations made in this Report. It requests the Commonwealth Secretariat to develop an appropriate framework for providing progress reports to Commonwealth Heads of Government at their biennial summits.

214. This Report is a call for responsibility, partnership and concrete actions – from governments, from firms, from civil society and from the international community. Without responsibility on all these levels, development and democracy will remain rhetoric rather than become reality. While development and democracy are goals in their own right, they can and should be mutually reinforcing. To promote peace and prosperity, Commonwealth Heads of Government must commit to a new, deeper approach to development and democracy.

End Notes

[1] Rao 2002, 1, 68-70.

[2] Quoted in Commonwealth Human Rights Initiative 2001.

[3] This list of capabilities appears in Office of the High Commissioner for Human Rights 2002, para. 47. See also Rao 2002, para. 5-6; UNDP 1990, 9; and Sen 1999, Ch. 4.

[4] Commonwealth Foundation 2002, 3.

[5] Office of the High Commissioner for Human Rights 2002, para. 48-51; Commonwealth Human Rights Initiative 2002, 2.

[6] The 'Washington Consensus' refers to a set of ten market-oriented policy objectives including, among others: fiscal discipline, trade liberalisation, privatisation of state enterprises, openness to foreign direct investment, and competitive exchange rates. See Rao 2002, Annex IV.

[7] This is the position of Joseph Stiglitz and many other analysts (Rao 2002, para. 123-133).

[8] In addition to the Harare and Fancourt Declarations, the perspective on democracy in this Report reflects the discussion of democracy in a number of other sources. See UNDP 2002, 4; Foweraker and Krznaric 2000, 770-774; Rao 2002, para. 105; Boutros-Ghali et al 2002; and Singh 1999, 1, On the importance of participation and civic associationalism see Commonwealth Foundation 1999; Knight, Chigudu and Tandon 2002; and Narayan et al 2000, 266-277. On local democracy see Commonwealth Local Government Forum 2002. On social and economic rights see Donnelly 1989, Ch. 2. On gender see Commonwealth Human Rights Initiative 2002. On group rights see Kymlicka 1995.

[9] As the ideas of both democracy and development have become broader, they increasingly overlap. Hence realising social and economic rights in practice may be part of the democratic ideal, but also contributes to development through helping provide basic capabilities. Similarly, capabilities such as equitable access to justice are often associated with civil and political rights.

[10] The extension of democracy into these arenas is discussed further below. On the idea of 'arenas' of democracy, see Linz and Stepan 1996, 7-15.

[11] These figures are based on assessments of Freedom House democracy indicators. See Diamond 1997, 22; UNDP 2002, 15.

[12] UNDP 2002, 13; Foweraker and Krznaric 2002.

[13] Narayan et al 2000.

[14] Quoted in Commonwealth Local Government Forum 2002.

[15] Data on development and democracy in the Commonwealth can be found in Appendix C.

[16] Rueschemeyer, Stephens and Stephens 1992, Ch. 2; Diamond 1999, Ch. 3; UNDP 2002, Ch. 2; Rao 2002, para. 86-103.

[17] Data for 1999 from UNDP 2002, 17-18. See also Rao 2002, para. 7-15.

[18] World Bank 2002, 183.

[19] Rao 2002, para. 37.

[20] The following data appear in Commonwealth Human Rights Initiative 2001, 4-15. See Appendices A and C for further data on poverty in the Commonwealth.

[21] These figures are based on estimates by the Commonwealth Policy Studies Unit's project 'Indigenous Rights in the Commonwealth'. 'Indigenous peoples' refers to communities, peoples and nations that, "having a historical continuity with pre-invasion and pre-colonial societies that developed in their territories, consider themselves distinct from other sectors of the societies now prevailing in those territories, or parts of them", and that currently form non-dominant sectors of society and aim to preserve their ethnic identity, cultural patterns, social institutions and legal systems. See Bourne 2003, 3, 5 and Whall (forthcoming).

[22] See UNDP 2003. The classification criteria are discussed in detail on pp. 347-349 of the report. There are some small differences between the presentation of data here and in the *Human Development Report*. Where UNDP labels progress as *slow or reversing* this report uses *slow*. Where UNDP classifies a country as being neither *top priority* nor *high priority* it labels the priority status as *other*, whereas this report uses *low priority*. See Appendix A for an outline of the classification system and for the full data used to construct these tables.

[23] Further analysis of the Millennium Development Goals appears in World Bank and International Monetary Fund 2003.

[24] The importance of an effective state and well-trained public officials is discussed in Singh 1999, 4-5. On the problem of corruption see Rao 2002, para. 108-117; Tanzi 1998, 571-573; Commonwealth Business Council 2002, 42-46; and Hawley 2003. See also the Report of the Commonwealth Expert Group on Good Governance and the Elimination of Corruption, Commonwealth Secretariat 2000.

[25] UNDP 2001, Ch. 4; Rao 2002, para. 205-208.

[26] Rao 2002, para. 197.

[27] Oxfam 2002a, 241; Rao 2002, para. 41.

[28] Rao 2002, para. 43-49; Commonwealth Human Rights Initiative 2001, 35-36.

[29] Commonwealth Secretariat 2001, 29.

[30] De Soto 2000; Rao 2002, para. 127, 131.

[31] Rao 2002, 207.

[32] Narayan et al 2000, 276-278.

[33] Oxfam 2002a, 8.

[34] Oxfam 2002a, 140-141.

[35] Quoted in Rao 2002, para. 154.

[36] Third World Network 2001, 23-24; Oxfam 2002a, 59.

[37] IMF and World Bank 2002, 23-25; Oxfam 2002b.

[38] McKinnon 2002, 7.

[39] Oxfam 2002a, Ch. 8.

[40] Lall 1997, Ch. 5.

[41] Oxfam 2002a, 178.

[42] See, for example, Commonwealth Business Council 2002, 26.

[43] The Commonwealth Business Council's principles and strategies for the promotion of corporate citizenship are set out in its publication 'Business in Society: Good Corporate Citizenship in the Commonwealth'. See also Commonwealth Business Council 2002.
[44] Rao 2002, para. 116.
[45] Peter Eigen quoted in Hawley 2003, 1.
[46] UNDP 2002, 68.
[47] Commonwealth Business Council 2002, 34-35.
[48] Dahl 1989, 328-332.
[49] On micro-credit schemes, see Rao 2002, para. 140.
[50] Johnson and Bartlett 2002.
[51] Mistry 2001, para. 5.04.
[52] Monterrey Consensus 2002, para. 20.
[53] Commonwealth Secretariat 1999.
[54] Singh 1999, 2-3.
[55] Commonwealth Secretariat 1997, xi; Hughes and Brewster, vii.
[56] Commonwealth Secretariat 1997, xi.
[57] Commonwealth Secretariat 2001, 24-25; Commonwealth Secretariat 2000.
[58] Rao 2002, para. 181.
[59] Rao 2002, para. 181; Birdsall and Deese 2002.
[60] International Development Association and International Monetary Fund 2003.
[61] Birdsall and Deese 2002, para. 5.
[62] Rao 2002, para. 181-184; Birdsall and Deese 2002, para. 17.
[63] These last two points appear in Khor 2002, 49-53. See also Akyüz 2002, 13.
[64] UNCTAD 2002, 214-215, 217.
[65] Rao 2002, para. 168.
[66] The Reality of Aid 2002, 128.
[67] UNCTAD 2002, 215
[68] Global Financial Governance Initiative 2002.
[69] HM Treasury 2002.
[70] UNCTAD 2002, 219; Rao 2002, para. 176-180.
[71] International Development Association and International Monetary Fund 2003, 13.
[72] UNCTAD 2002, 170, 191-193; Oxfam 2002a, 143-146; Wilks and Lefrançois 2002.
[73] Rao 2002, para. 171.
[74] Rao 2002, para. 173; Narayan et al 2000, 132-142; Mistry 2001, para. 5.58.
[75] Office of the High Commissioner for Human Rights 2002, para. 205.
[76] Rao 2002, para. 180.
[77] UNDP 2002, 113-114. See also Rao 2002, para. 209-218.
[78] Some of these critiques appear in UNDP 2002, 113-114 and Khor 2002, 46-47.
[79] International Monetary Fund and World Bank 2003, 1-6.
[80] Rao 2002, para. 17 based on data from The Stockholm International Peace Research Institute.
[81] UNDP 2002, 85.

[82] Rao 2002, 67.
[83] Rao 2002, para. 81.
[84] Nield 1999; UNDP 2002, 94.
[85] Commonwealth Human Rights Initiative 2001, 38.
[86] Rao 2002, para. 20-25.
[87] Commonwealth Human Rights Initiative 2001, 36-38.
[88] Baksh-Sooden and Etchart 2002.
[89] International Network on Cultural Policy 2002, Executive Summary para. 6.
[90] Commonwealth Human Rights Initiative 2002, 3.
[91] UNDP 2002, 94.

References

Akyüz, Yilmaz (2002). 'Towards Reform of the International Financial Architecture: Which way forward?' in Yilmaz Akyüz (ed.), *Reforming the Global Financial Architecture: Issues and Proposals,* Penang, Malaysia: Third World Network, Geneva: UNCTAD, and London and New York: Zed Books.

Baksh-Sooden, Rawwida and Linda Etchart (eds.) (2002). *Women and Men in Partnership for Post-Conflict Reconstruction: Report of the Sierra Leone National Consultation, Freetown, Sierra Leone, 21-24 May 2001,* London: Commonwealth Secretariat.

Birdsall, Nancy and Michael Clemens (2003). 'From Promise to Performance: How rich countries can help poor countries help themselves', *CDG Brief,* Vol. 2, Issue 1, April, www.cgdev.org

Birdsall, Nancy and Brian Deese (2002). 'Beyond HIPC: Secure sustainable debt relief for poor countries', August, London: Commonwealth Secretariat.

Bourne, Richard (2003). 'Invisible Lives: Undercounted, underrepresented and underneath: The socioeconomic plight of indigenous peoples in the Commonwealth', Indigenous Rights in the Commonwealth Project, London: Commonwealth Policy Studies Unit.

Boutros-Ghali, Boutros et al (2002). *The Interaction between Democracy and Development,* Paris: UNESCO.

Budlender, Debbie (2000). 'The Political Economy of Women's Budgets in the South', London: Commonwealth Secretariat.

_____, Janine Hicks and Lisa Vetten (2002). 'South Africa: Expanding into diverse initiatives' in Debbie Budlender and Guy Hewitt (eds.), *Gender Budgets Make More Cents: Country Studies and Good Practice,* London: Commonwealth Secretariat.

Commonwealth Business Council (2002). 'COMPAC, Commonwealth Principles for Action: A 16 point programme for investment', January, London: Commonwealth Business Council.

Commonwealth Foundation (2002). 'Civil Society Consultation on the 2002 Commonwealth Finance Ministers Meeting, London, United Kingdom, 22-23 July 2002: Report of the Meeting', September, London: Commonwealth Foundation.

_____ (1999). *Citizens and Governance: Civil Society in the New Millennium*, London: Commonwealth Foundation.

Commonwealth Human Rights Initiative (CHRI) (2002). 'Submission to the Expert Group on Democracy and Development, London, November 11th, 2002', New Delhi: CHRI.

_____ (2001). 'Human Rights and Poverty Eradication: A talisman for the Commonwealth', New Delhi: CHRI.

Commonwealth Local Government Forum (2002). 'Submission by the Commonwealth Local Government Forum to the Commonwealth Expert Group on Democracy and Development', London.

Commonwealth Secretariat (2001). 'Report of the Commonwealth Secretary-General 2001: Continuity and renewal in the new millennium', London: Commonwealth Secretariat.

_____ (2000). 'Fighting Corruption, Promoting Good Governance: Report of the Commonwealth Expert Group on Good Governance and the Elimination of Corruption', London: Commonwealth Secretariat.

_____ (1999). 'Commonwealth Code of Good Practice for Promoting Private Flows and Coping with Capital Market Volatility', London: Commonwealth Secretariat.

_____ (1997). 'A Future for Small States: Overcoming vulnerability – Report by a Commonwealth Advisory Group', London: Commonwealth Secretariat.

Dahl, Robert A (1989). *Democracy and its Critics*, New Haven and London: Yale University Press.

De Soto, Hernando (2000). *The Mystery of Capital: Why Capitalism Triumphs in the West and Fails Everywhere Else*, London: Bantam Press.

Diamond, Larry (1999). *Developing Democracy: Toward Consolidation*, Baltimore and London: Johns Hopkins University Press.

_____ (1997). 'The End of the Third Wave and the Global Future of Democracy', Reihe Polikwissenschaft/Political Science Series No. 45, July, Vienna: Institute for Advanced Studies.

Dodhia, Dinesh (2002). 'Progress Report on Implementing the HIPC Initiative', August, London: Commonwealth Secretariat.

Donnelly, Jack (1989). *Universal Human Rights in Theory and Practice*, Ithaca and London: Cornell University Press.

Global Financial Governance Initiative (2002). 'Report on the Third Meeting October 11, 2002 at the Carnegie Endowment for International Peace, Washington', Global Financial Governance Initiative Working Group Number Three on Institutional Reform in Global Financial Governance, chaired by Ngaire Woods.

International Monetary Fund and World Bank (2002). 'Market Access for Developing Country Exports: Selected issues', 26 September, Washington DC: IMF and World Bank.

Foweraker, Joe and Roman Krznaric (2002). 'The Uneven Performance of Third Wave Democracies: Electoral politics and the imperfect rule of law in Latin America', *Latin American Politics and Society*, Vol. 44, No. 3: 29-60.

_____ (2000). 'Measuring Liberal Democratic Performance: An empirical and conceptual critique', *Political Studies*, Vol. 48, No. 4: 759-787.

Hawley, Susan (2003). 'Export Credit and Corruption: The UK's Export Credit Guarantee Department', The Corner House, www.thecornerhouse.org.uk

HM Treasury (2002). 'International Financing Facility', December, London: HM Treasury, www.hm-treasury.gov.uk/mediastore/otherfiles/International%20Finance%20Facil.pdf

Hughes, Anthony and Havelock Brewster (2002). 'Lowering the Threshold: Reducing the cost and risk of private direct investment in least developed, small and vulnerable economies', London: Commonwealth Secretariat.

International Development Association and International Monetary Fund (2003). 'Update on Implementation of Action Plans to Strengthen Capacity of HIPCs to Track Poverty: Reducing public spending', March, Washington DC: World Bank and International Monetary Fund.

International Monetary Fund and World Bank (2003). 'Enhancing the Voice and Participation of Developing and Transition Countries in Decision-making at the World Bank and IMF', Technical Note by Bank/Fund Staff for the Development Committee, 27 March, Washington, DC: International Monetary Fund and World Bank.

International Network on Cultural Policy (2002). 'Cultural Diversity in Developing Countries: The challenges of globalisation', October, www.incp-ricp.org

Jenkins, Roy and Anne-Marie Goetz (1999). 'Constraints on Civil Society's Capacity to Curb Corruption: Lessons from the Indian experience', *IDS Bulletin*, Vol. 30, No. 4: 39-49.

Johnson, Tina and Jane Bartlett (2002). *Commonwealth Businesswomen: Trade Matters, Best Practices and Success Stories*, London: Commonwealth Secretariat.

Khor, Martin (2002). 'The WTO, the Post-Doha Agenda and the Future of the Trade System: A development perspective', Penang, Malaysia: Third World Network.

Knight, Barry, Hope Chigudu and Rajesh Tandon (2002). *Reviving Democracy: Citizens at the Heart of Governance*, London and Sterling, VA: Earthscan.

Kymlicka, Will (1995). *Multicultural Citizenship: A Liberal Theory of Minority Rights*, Oxford: Clarendon Press.

Lall, Sanjaya (1997). 'Attracting Foreign Investment: New trends, sources and policies', Economic Paper 31, London: Commonwealth Secretariat.

Linz, Juan J and Alfred Stepan (1996). *Problems of Democratic Transition and Consolidation: Southern Europe, South America, and Post-Communist Europe*, Baltimore and London: Johns Hopkins University Press.

McKinnon, Don (2002). 'Opening Remarks by the Commonwealth Secretary-General, Rt Hon Don McKinnon', Commonwealth Expert Group on Development and Democracy, 11-12 November 2002, Commonwealth Secretariat, Marlborough House, London.

Mistry, Percy (2001). 'Financing for Development: Perspectives and issues', August, London: Commonwealth Secretariat.

Monterrey Consensus (2002). Adopted by Heads of Government at the UN Financing for Development Conference in Monterrey, Mexico, 22 March 2002, http://usinfo.state.gov/topical/gobal/develop/02032205.htm

Narayan, Deepa et al (2000). *Voices of the Poor: Can Anyone Hear Us?*, Washington DC: World Bank and New York: Oxford University Press.

Nield, Rachel (1999). 'From National Rights to Citizen Rights: Civil society and the evolution of public order debates', International Centre for Human Rights and Democratic Development, www.ichrdd.ca/111/ english/c.../publications/citizensecurity.html.

Office of the High Commissioner for Human Rights (OHCHR) (2002). 'Draft Guidelines: A human rights approach to poverty reduction strategies', Geneva: OHCHR.

Organisation for Economic Co-operation and Development (2000). 'OECD Guidelines for Multinational Enterprises', www.itcilo.it/english.actrav/telearn/global/ilo/guide/oecd.htm

Oxfam (2002a). *Rigged Rules and Double Standards: Trade, Globalisation and the Fight against Poverty*, Oxford: Oxfam International.

———— (2002b). 'The Great EU Sugar Scam: How Europe's sugar regime is devastating livelihoods in the developing world', Oxfam Briefing Paper 27, August, Oxford: Oxfam International.

Rao, Siriparapu K (2002). 'Commonwealth Expert Group on Democracy and Development: Background note on issues for its consideration', October, London: Commonwealth Secretariat.

The Reality of Aid (2002). *The Reality of Aid 2002*, www.devint.org/ktrends.pdf

Ronsholt, Frans (2002). 'Country Report – Tanzania, OECD-DAC Study on donor burdens and good practices', draft, 27 July, www.tzdac.or.tz

Roy, Bunker (2000). 'Villages as a Positive Force for Good Governance: The right to information and India's struggle against grass-roots corruption', *United Nations Chronicle Online Edition*, Vol. XXXVII, No. 1, Department of Public Information, www.un.org/Pubs/chronicle/2000/issue1/100p86.htm

Rueschemeyer, Dietrich, Evelyne Huber Stephens and John D Stephens (1992). *Capitalist Development and Democracy*, Cambridge: Polity Press.

Sen, Amartya (1999). *Development as Freedom*, New York: Alfred A. Knopf.

Singh, Manmohan (1999). 'Democracy and Development: The political foundation of a market economy', address at the First Conference on Democracy, Centre for Policy Research, New Delhi, 15 February.

Tanzi, Vito (1998). 'Corruption Around the World: Causes, consequences, scope and cures', *IMF Staff Papers*, Vol. 45, No. 4, December: 559-594.

Third World Network (2001). 'The Multilateral Trading System: A development perspective', December, New York: United Nations Development Programme.

United Nations Conference on Trade and Development (2002). *The Least Developed Countries Report 2002: Escaping the Poverty Trap,* New York and Geneva: United Nations.

United Nations Development Programme (2003). *Human Development Report*, New York: Oxford University Press.

_____ (2002). *Human Development Report*, New York: Oxford University Press.

_____ (2001). *Human Development Report*, New York: Oxford University Press.

_____ (1990). *Human Development Report*, Oxford: Oxford University Press.

Watkins, Kevin (2000). *The Oxfam Education Report,* Oxford: Oxfam.

Whall, Helena (forthcoming). 'Indigenous Peoples in the Commonwealth: A story of exclusion', *The Parliamentarian*, Commonwealth Parliamentary Association, www.cpahq.org.

Wilks, Alex and Fabien Lefrançois (2002). 'Blinding with Science or Encouraging Debate? How World Bank analysis determines PRSP policies', London: Bretton Woods Project and Monrovia, CA: World Vision International.

World Bank (2002). *World Development Report 2003: Sustainable Development in a Dynamic World,* Washington DC: World Bank.

World Bank and International Monetary Fund (2003). 'Achieving the MDGs and Related Outcomes: A framework for monitoring policies and actions', 28 March, Washington DC: Development Committee, World Bank and International Monetary Fund.

Appendix A: Progress towards the Millennium Development Goals in Commonwealth Countries

The Millennium Development Goals (MDGs) were adopted by the UN General Assembly in September 2000. Each of the eight Goals is accompanied by targets to be achieved by 2015 (see Appendix B). The Goals are to: (1) eradicate extreme poverty and hunger; (2) achieve universal primary education; (3) promote gender equality and empower women; (4) reduce child mortality; (5) improve maternal health; (6) combat HIV/AIDS, malaria and other diseases; (7) ensure environmental sustainability; and (8) develop a global partnership for development.

The following tables review the progress of Commonwealth countries towards the MDGs and provide an assessment of which countries require priority attention with respect both to the achievement of each Goal and to the Goals overall. The tables are based on data and classifications that appear in the United Nations Development Programme's *Human Development Report 2003*. Summaries of these tables appear in the main text (Tables 1 and 2).

Defining progress towards each Goal

The following criteria are used to define a country's progress towards each Goal:

Rate of progress	Definition
Slow	Actual progress towards the Goal is *less than half* the approximate progress required to meet the target if current trends prevail until 2015. Progress is thus slow or possibly reversing.
Moderate	Actual progress towards the Goal is *more than half but less than* the approximate progress required to meet the target if current trends prevail until 2015.
Fast	Actual progress towards the Goal *is equal to or greater than* the approximate progress required to meet the target if current trends prevail until 2015.

Note: The year in which the target is to be met is 2015 for all except gender equality in education, for which it is 2005.

Assessing countries as *top priority*, *high priority* and *low priority* for each Goal

For each MDG the priority assessment of a country is based both on its progress towards the Goal (*slow*, *moderate* or *fast*) and on its level of human poverty in the Goal (*extreme*, *medium* or *low*). Progress is measured against the targets and using the indicators defined for the MDGs:

- A country is designated *top priority* for a Goal if it has both extreme human poverty in that goal and slow progress towards it. In these countries urgent action is required to meet the goal. *Top priority* countries are highlighted in the tables.

- A country is designated *high priority* for a Goal if it has both extreme human poverty in that Goal and moderate progress towards it **or** if it has medium human poverty in that Goal and slow progress towards it. In these countries the situation is less desperate but still demands significant improvements in progress.

- A country is designated *low priority* for a Goal if it has some other combination of human poverty in the Goal and progress towards it.

	Level of human poverty in Goal	Slow	Moderate	Fast
	Low	Low priority	Low priority	Low priority
	Medium	**High priority**	Low priority	Low priority
	Extreme	*Top priority*	**High priority**	Low priority

Progress towards Goal

1. Priority status and progress towards the MDGs for Commonwealth countries (all MDGs and Goals 1-3)

	Priority status across all the MDGs	Goal 1: Eradicate extreme poverty and hunger — Target: Halve the proportion of people living on under $1/day				Goal 2: Achieve universal primary education — Target: Ensure all children can complete primary education		Goal 3: Promote gender equality and empower women — Target: Eliminate gender disparity in all levels of education by 2005	
		Population living below $1/day (%)		Undernourished people (% population)		Net primary enrolment ratio (%)		Ratio of girls to boys in primary and secondary education (%)	
		Priority	Progress	Priority	Progress	Priority	Progress	Priority	Progress
Antigua and Barbuda	..	Low	Fast	..	..	..	..	..	a
Australia	Low	Low	Fast	..	..	Low	Slow	Low	a
Bahamas, The	High	..	..	..	..	High	Slow	Low	a
Bangladesh	Low	Low	Slow	Top	Slow	Low	Moderate	Low	a
Barbados	Low	Low	Fast	..	..	Low	Moderate	..	a
Belize	Low	Low	Moderate	..	..	Low	Slow	Low	a
Botswana	High	Low	Fast	High	Slow	High	Slow	Low	a
Brunei Darussalam	..	..	..	..	..	..	..	Low	a
Cameroon	Top	Top	Slow	Low	Fast	..	..	High	a
Canada	Low	Low	Fast	..	..	Low	Slow	Low	a
Cyprus	Low	Low	Fast	..	..	Low	Slow	Low	a
Dominica	..	Low	Moderate	..	..	..	..	..	a
Fiji Islands	Low	Low	Moderate	..	..	Low	Slow	..	a
Gambia, The	High	Top	Slow	High	Slow	High	Moderate	Low	a
Ghana	Low	Low	Slow	Low	Fast	..	..	..	a
Grenada	..	Low	Moderate	..	..	..	..	..	a
Guyana	Low	Low	Moderate	Low	Fast	Low	Slow	..	a
India	High	Low	Slow	High	Slow	..	..	High	a
Jamaica	Low	High	Moderate	Low	Fast	Low	Slow	Low	a

	Priority status across all the MDGs	Goal 1: Eradicate extreme poverty and hunger				Goal 2: Achieve universal primary education		Goal 3: Promote gender equality and empower women	
		Target: Halve the proportion of people living on under $1/day		Target: Halve the proportion of people suffering from hunger		Target: Ensure all children can complete primary education		Target: Eliminate gender disparity in all levels of education by 2005	
		Population living below $1/day (%)		Undernourished people (% population)		Net primary enrolment ratio (%)		Ratio of girls to boys in primary and secondary education (%)	
		Priority	Progress	Priority	Progress	Priority	Progress	Priority	Progress
Kenya	Top	Top	Slow	Top	Slow	..	..	..	a
Kiribati	..	..	..	..	..	..	..	..	a
Lesotho	Top	Low	Slow	Top	Slow	Low	Slow	Low	a
Malawi	High	Low	Slow	Low	Fast	Low	Fast	Low	a
Malaysia	Low	Low	Fast	..	..	..	..	Low	a
Maldives	..	..	..	..	..	..	..	..	a
Malta	Low	Low	Fast	..	..	Low	Slow	Low	a
Mauritius	Low	Low	Fast	Low	Fast	Low	Slow	Low	a
Mozambique	Top	Low	Slow	Low	Fast	Top	Slow	Top	a
Namibia	High	Low	Fast	Low	Fast	High	Slow	Low	a
Nauru	..	..	..	..	..	..	..	..	a
New Zealand	Low	Low	Fast	..	..	Low	Slow	Low	a
Nigeria	Top	Top	Slow	Low	Fast	..	..	..	a
Pakistan	Low	High	Slow	Low	Fast	..	..	..	a
Papua New Guinea	High	High	Slow	Top	Slow	..	..	Low	a
Saint Kitts and Nevis	..	Low	Fast	..	..	..	..	..	a
Saint Lucia	Low	High	Moderate	..	..	..	..	Low	a
Saint Vincent and the Grenadines	..	Low	Moderate	..	..	..	..	..	a
Samoa	Low	Low	Moderate	..	..	..	..	Low	a
Seychelles	..	..	..	..	..	..	..	..	a

	Priority status across all the MDGs	Goal 1: Eradicate extreme poverty and hunger				Goal 2: Achieve universal primary education		Goal 3: Promote gender equality and empower women	
		Target: Halve the proportion of people living on under $1/day		Target: Halve the proportion of people suffering from hunger		Target: Ensure all children can complete primary education		Target: Eliminate gender disparity in all levels of education by 2005	
		Population living below $1/day (%)		Undernourished people (% population)		Net primary enrolment ratio (%)		Ratio of girls to boys in primary and secondary education (%)	
		Priority	Progress	Priority	Progress	Priority	Progress	Priority	Progress
Sierra Leone	Top	Top	Slow	Top	Slow	..	..	Top	a
Singapore	Low	Low	Fast	..	..	..	..	..	a
Solomon Islands	..	Top	Slow	..	..	..	..	..	a
South Africa	High	Low	Fast	..	..	High	Slow	Low	a
Sri Lanka	Low	Low	Slow	Low	Fast	..	..	Low	a
Swaziland	High	High	Moderate	High	Slow	Low	Slow	..	a
Tanzania, U. Rep. of	Top	Top	Slow	Top	Slow	Top	Slow	Low	a
Tonga	..	..	..	..	..	..	..	Low	a
Trinidad and Tobago	Low	Low	Fast	High	Slow	Low	Slow	Low	a
Tuvalu	..	..	..	..	..	..	..	..	a
Uganda	Low	Low	Slow	Low	Moderate	..	..	..	a
United Kingdom	Low	Low	Fast	..	..	Low	Slow	Low	a
Vanuatu	Low	Low	Slow	..	..	..	..	Low	a
Zambia	Top	Top	Slow	Top	Slow	..	..	..	a
Zimbabwe	Top	Top	Slow	High	Moderate	..	..	Low	a

Note: **a** Progress classification unavailable.

2. Priority status and progress towards the MDGs for Commonwealth countries (Goals 4 and 7)

	Goal 4: Reduce child mortality		Goal 7: Ensure environmental sustainability			
	Target: Reduce under-five infant mortality rates by two thirds		Target: Halve the proportion of people without sustainable access to safe drinking water		Target: Achieve a significant improvement in the lives of at least 100m slum dwellers	
	Under-five mortality rate (per 1000 live births)		People with access to improved water sources (%)		People with access to adequate sanitation (%)	
	Priority	Progress	Priority	Progress	Priority	Progress
Antigua and Barbuda	..	..	..	..	..	..
Australia	Low	Fast	Low	Slow	Low	Slow
Bahamas, The	Low	Fast	..	..	..	..
Bangladesh	Low	Fast	Low	Fast	High	Moderate
Barbados	Low	Slow	..	..	..	..
Belize	Low	Moderate	..	..	..	..
Botswana	Top	Slow	Low	Fast	High	Moderate
Brunei Darussalam	Low	Fast	..	..	..	..
Cameroon	Top	Slow	High	Moderate	Top	Slow
Canada	Low	Slow	Low	Slow	Low	Slow
Cyprus	Low	Fast	Low	Slow	Low	Slow
Dominica	Low	Fast	..	..	..	..
Fiji Islands	Low	Fast	..	..	..	..
Gambia, The	High	Moderate	..	..	..	..
Ghana	Low	Moderate	Low	Fast	Low	Fast
Grenada	Low	Fast	..	..	..	..
Guyana	Low	Moderate	..	..	..	..
India	Low	Moderate	Low	Fast	High	Moderate
Jamaica	Low	Slow	Low	Slow	Low	Slow

	Goal 4: Reduce child mortality		Goal 7: Ensure environmental sustainability			
	Target: Reduce under-five infant mortality rates by two thirds		Target: Halve the proportion of people without sustainable access to safe drinking water		Target: Achieve a significant improvement in the lives of at least 100m slum dwellers	
	Under-five mortality rate (per 1000 live births)		People with access to improved water sources (%)		People with access to adequate sanitation (%)	
	Priority	Progress	Priority	Progress	Priority	Progress
Kenya	Top	Slow	Low	Fast	Low	Fast
Kiribati	Low	Moderate	..	..	..	..
Lesotho	Top	Slow	..	..	..	..
Malawi	High	Moderate	High	Moderate	High	Moderate
Malaysia	Low	Fast	..	..	..	..
Maldives	Low	Fast	..	..	..	..
Malta	Low	Fast	Low	Slow	Low	Slow
Mauritius	Low	Moderate	Low	Slow	..	..
Mozambique	High	Moderate	..	..	..	..
Namibia	Low	Moderate	High	Moderate	High	Moderate
Nauru	..	..	..	..	..	..
New Zealand	Low	Fast	High	Moderate	Top	Slow
Nigeria	Top	Slow	Low	Fast	Low	Fast
Pakistan	High	Moderate	Top	Slow	High	Slow
Papua New Guinea	High	Slow	..	..	..	..
Saint Kitts and Nevis	Low	Fast	..	..	..	..
Saint Lucia	Low	Moderate	..	..	..	..
Saint Vincent and the Grenadines	Low	Slow	..	..	..	..
Samoa	Low	Fast	..	..	..	..
Seychelles	Low	Moderate	..	..	..	..

	Goal 4: Reduce child mortality			Goal 7: Ensure environmental sustainability			
	Target: Reduce under-five infant mortality rates by two thirds			Target: Halve the proportion of people without sustainable access to safe drinking water		Target: Achieve a significant improvement in the lives of at least 100m slum dwellers	
	Under-five mortality rate (per 1000 live births)			People with access to improved water sources (%)		People with access to adequate sanitation (%)	
	Priority	Progress		Priority	Progress	Priority	Progress
Sierra Leone	Top	Slow		..	..	..	..
Singapore	Low	Fast		Low	Slow	Low	Slow
Solomon Islands	Low	Fast		..	..	..	..
South Africa	High	Slow		High	Slow	High	Slow
Sri Lanka	Low	Moderate		Low	Fast	Low	Fast
Swaziland	Top	Slow		..	..	..	..
Tanzania, U. Rep. of	Top	Slow		Low	Fast	Low	Fast
Tonga	Low	Moderate		..	..	..	..
Trinidad and Tobago	Low	Moderate		Low	Slow	Low	Slow
Tuvalu	..	..		..	Moderate	..	..
Uganda	High	Moderate		High	Slow	Low	Slow
United Kingdom	Low	Moderate		Low	Slow	Low	Slow
Vanuatu	Low	Fast		..	..	..	..
Zambia	Top	Slow		Low	Fast	Low	Fast
Zimbabwe	Top	Slow		Low	Fast	High	Moderate

4. Data on progress towards the MDGs for Commonwealth countries (Goals 4 and 7)

	Goal 4: Reduce child mortality		Goal 7: Ensure environmental sustainability			
	Target: Reduce under-five infant mortality rates by two thirds		Target: Halve the proportion of people without sustainable access to safe drinking water		Target: Achieve a significant improvement in the lives of at least 100m slum dwellers	
	Under-five mortality rate (per 1000 live births)		People with access to improved water sources (%)		People with access to adequate sanitation (%)	
	1990	2001	1990	2000	1990	2000
Antigua and Barbuda	..	14	..	91	..	95
Australia	10	6	100	100	100	100
Bahamas, The	29	16	..	97	..	100
Bangladesh	144	77	94	97	41	48
Barbados	16	14	..	100	..	100
Belize	49	40	..	92	..	50
Botswana	58	110	93	95	60	66
Brunei Darussalam	11	6	..	..	..	..
Cameroon	139	155	51	58	77	79
Canada	8	7	100	100	100	100
Cyprus	12	6	100	100	100	100
Dominica	23	15	..	97	..	83
Fiji Islands	31	21	..	47	..	43
Gambia, The	154	126	..	62	..	37
Ghana	126	100	53	73	61	72
Grenada	37	25	..	95	..	97
Guyana	90	72	..	94	..	87
India	123	93	68	84	16	28
Jamaica	20	20	93	92	99	99

92   MAKING DEMOCRACY WORK FOR PRO-POOR DEVELOPMENT

	Goal 1: Eradicate extreme poverty and hunger					Goal 2: Achieve universal primary education		Goal 3: Promote gender equality and empower women	
	Target: Halve the proportion of people living on under $1/day		Target: Halve the proportion of people suffering from hunger			Target: Ensure that all children can complete primary education		Target: Eliminate gender disparity in all levels of education by 2005	
	Population living below $1/day (%)		*Undernourished people (% population)*			*Net primary enrolment ratio (%)*		*Ratio of girls to boys in primary and secondary education (%)*	
	1990	2001	1990e	2000f		1990	2000	1990	2000
Sierra Leone	913	470	46	47		..	..	67	77
Singapore	14,737	22,680	..	..		..	..	89.0	..
Solomon Islands	2,427	1,910	..	..		..	..	77.1	..
South Africa	11,414	11,290	..	..		102.6 a	88.9	103	100
Sri Lanka	2,235	3,180	29	23		..	97.0 c	99	102 c
Swaziland	4,365	4,330	10	12		87.9	92.8	..	95.7 d
Tanzania, U. Rep. of	498	520	36	47		51.4	46.7	97	99
Tonga	..	..	..	..		..	91.5	92	102
Trinidad and Tobago	6,708	9,100	13	12		90.9	92.4	98	102
Tuvalu	..	..	..	..		..	..	..	..
Uganda	1,055	1,490	23	21		..	109.5	..	88.9
United Kingdom	19,236.8	24,160.0	..	..		97.0	98.9	97	111
Vanuatu	3,501	3,190	..	..		..	95.9	86 a	102
Zambia	919	780	45	50		..	65.5	..	92.4
Zimbabwe	2,666	2,280	43	38		..	79.6	96	94

Note: **a** Refers to 1991. **b** Refers to 1992. **c** Refers to 1998. **d** Refers to 1999. **e** Average 1990-1992. **f** Average 1998-2000.

	Goal 1: Eradicate extreme poverty and hunger				Goal 2: Achieve universal primary education		Goal 3: Promote gender equality and empower women	
	Target: Halve the proportion of people living on under $1/day		Target: Halve the proportion of people suffering from hunger		Target: Ensure that all children can complete primary education		Target: Eliminate gender disparity in all levels of education by 2005	
	GDP per capita (PPP US$)		Undernourished people (% population)		Net primary enrolment ratio (%)		Ratio of girls to boys in primary and secondary education (%)	
	1990	2001	1990e	2000f	1990	2000	1990	2000
Kenya	1,079	980	47	44	..	68.5	..	97.2
Kiribati	..	..	..	..	..	..	97.9	..
Lesotho	1,953	2,420	27	26	72.8	78.4	124	107
Malawi	508	570	49	33	49.7	100.6	79	94
Malaysia	5,769	8,750	3	..	..	98.5	98	105
Maldives	..	..	..	..	..	99.0	..	101.0
Malta	9,000.3	13,160	..	..	98.6	99.1 d	90	101 d
Mauritius	6,378	9,860	6	5	94.9	94.7	98	97
Mozambique	743	1,140	69	55	46.8	54.4	73	75
Namibia	5,764	7,120	15	9	89.4 b	81.6	111	104
Nauru	..	..	..	..	..	..	..	..
New Zealand	15,805.7	19,160	..	..	101.3	99.3	96	103
Nigeria	853	850	13	7	..	..	75.8	..
Pakistan	1,638	1,890	25	19	..	66.2	46.8	..
Papua New Guinea	2,200	2,570	25	27	..	83.8 d	77	90 d
Saint Kitts and Nevis	7,876	11,300	..	..	..	..	97.2 a	..
Saint Lucia	4,941	5,260	..	..	..	99.8	103	105
Saint Vincent and the Grenadines	4,222	5,330	..	..	..	..	104.2	..
Samoa	4,933	6,180	..	..	..	96.9	100	102
Seychelles	..	..	..	..	..	..	95.8 a	..

3. Data on progress towards the MDGs for Commonwealth countries (Goals 1-3)

	Goal 1: Eradicate extreme poverty and hunger					Goal 2: Achieve universal primary education		Goal 3: Promote gender equality and empower women	
	Target: Halve the proportion of people living on under $1/day				Target: Halve the proportion of people suffering from hunger	Target: Ensure that all children can complete primary education		Target: Eliminate gender disparity in all levels of education by 2005	
	GDP per capita (PPP US$)		Undernourished people (% population)			Net primary enrolment ratio (%)		Ratio of girls to boys in primary and secondary education (%)	
	1990	2001	1990e	2000f	1990	2000	1990	2000
Antigua and Barbuda	7,875	10,170	..	..	..	..	98.3 a	..
Australia	19,530.7	25,370	..	..	99.2	95.7	96	100
Bahamas, The	..	..	..	..	96.0 a	82.8 d	98 a	97 d
Bangladesh	1,160	1,610	35	35	64.0	88.9	72	103
Barbados	13,246	15,560	..	..	77.9 a	104.9	..	100.1
Belize	4,537	5,690	..	..	97.8 a	100.1	96	101
Botswana	5,809	7,820	17	25	93.3	84.3	107	102
Brunei Darussalam	..	..	..	..	91.0 a	..	94 a	100
Cameroon	1,822	1,680	32	25	..	..	82	81 c
Canada	22,602.8	27,130	..	..	96.9	98.6 d	94	101 d
Cyprus	15,152.3	21,190	..	..	86.9	94.9	95	101
Dominica	4,816	5,520	..	..	..	..	..	..
Fiji Islands	4,122	4,850	..	..	100.9 a	99.3 c	93.5	..
Gambia, The	1,993	2,050	21	21	50.9 a	68.7	64	85
Ghana	1,848	2,250	35	12	..	58.2	..	..
Grenada	5,315	6,740	..	..	..	84.2	91.6	88.2
Guyana	3,006	4,690	19	14	92.8	97.9 d	100.9	..
India	1,928	2,840	25	24	..	..	68 b	78 d
Jamaica	3,829	3,720	14	9	95.7	94.9	97	101

	Goal 4: Reduce child mortality		Goal 7: Ensure environmental sustainability			
	Target: Reduce under-five infant mortality rates by two thirds		Target: Halve the proportion of people without sustainable access to safe drinking water		Target: Achieve a significant improvement in the lives of at least 100m slum dwellers	
	Under-five mortality rate (per 1000 live births)		People with access to improved water sources (%)		People with access to adequate sanitation (%)	
	1990	2001	1990	2000	1990	2000
Kenya	97	122	45	57	80	87
Kiribati	88	69	..	48	..	48
Lesotho	148	132	..	78	..	49
Malawi	241	183	49	57	73	76
Malaysia	21	8	..	..	..	..
Maldives	115	77	..	100	..	56
Malta	14	5	100	100	100	100
Mauritius	25	19	100	100	100	99
Mozambique	235	197	..	57	..	43
Namibia	84	67	72	77	33	41
Nauru	..	..	..	..	..	..
New Zealand	11	6	..	..	..	..
Nigeria	190	183	53	62	53	54
Pakistan	128	109	83	90	36	62
Papua New Guinea	101	94	40	42	82	82
Saint Kitts and Nevis	36	24	..	98	..	96
Saint Lucia	24	19	..	98	..	89
Saint Vincent and the Grenadines	26	25	..	93	..	96
Samoa	42	25	..	99	..	99
Seychelles	21	17	..	..	..	..

	Goal 4: Reduce child mortality		Goal 7: Ensure environmental sustainability			
	Target: Reduce under-five infant mortality rates by two thirds		Target: Halve the proportion of people without sustainable access to safe drinking water		Target: Achieve a significant improvement in the lives of at least 100m slum dwellers	
	Under-five mortality rate (per 1000 live births)		*People with access to improved water sources (%)*		*People with access to adequate sanitation (%)*	
	1990	2001	1990	2000	1990	2000
Sierra Leone	323	316	..	57	..	66
Singapore	8	4	100	100	100	100
Solomon Islands	36	24	..	71	..	34
South Africa	60	71	86	86	86	87
Sri Lanka	23	19	68	77	85	94
Swaziland	110	149	..	..	..	..
Tanzania, U. Rep. of	163	165	38	68	84	90
Tonga	27	20	..	100	..	..
Trinidad and Tobago	24	20	91	90	99	99
Tuvalu	..	..	..	..	..	..
Uganda	165	124	45	52	..	79
United Kingdom	9	7	100	100	100	100
Vanuatu	70	42	..	88	..	100
Zambia	192	202	52	64	63	78
Zimbabwe	80	123	78	83	56	62

5: Progress towards MDG 8: Develop a global partnership for development

Target: Develop further an open, rules-based, predictable, non-discriminatory trading and financial system

		Australia	Canada	New Zealand	United Kingdom	DAC average
Net Official Development Assistance disbursed as % GNI	1990	0.34	0.44	0.23	0.27	**0.33**
	2001	0.25	0.22	0.25	0.32	**0.22**
Net Official Development Assistance disbursed to least developed countries as % GNI	1990	0.06	0.13	0.04	0.09	**0.09**
	2001	0.05	0.03	0.07	0.11	**0.05**
Country support to domestic agriculture as % GDP	1990	0.8	1.7	0.5	..	**1.9a**
	2001	0.3	0.7	0.3	..	**1.3a**
United bilateral Official Development Assistance as % of total	1990	33	47	100	..	**68**
	2001	59	32	..	94	**79**

Note: This table is based on data for members of the Development Assistance Committee (DAC) of the Organisation for Economic Co-operation and Development (OECD).
a OECD average using aggregate data for European Union countries.

Appendix B: The Millennium Development Goals, Targets and Indicators (Goals 1-6)

Goal 1: Eradicate extreme poverty and hunger	
Target 1: Halve, between 1990 and 2015, the proportion of people whose income is less than one dollar a day	Indicator 1. Proportion of population below $1 per day (PPP values) Indicator 2. Poverty gap ratio (incidence x depth of poverty) Indicator 3. Share of poorest quintile in national consumption
Target 2: Halve, between 1990 and 2015, the proportion of people who suffer from hunger	Indicator 4. Prevalence of underweight children under five years of age Indicator 5. Proportion of population below minimum level of dietary energy consumption

Goal 2: Achieve universal primary education	
Target 3: Ensure that, by 2015, children everywhere, boys and girls alike, will be able to complete a full course of primary schooling	Indicator 6. Net enrolment ratio in primary education Indicator 7. Proportion of pupils starting grade 1 who reach grade 5 Indicator 8. Literacy rate of 15-24 year olds

Goal 3: Promote gender equality and empower women	
Target 4: Eliminate gender disparity in primary and secondary education, preferably by 2005, and to all levels of education no later than 2015	Indicator 9. Ratios of girls to boys in primary, secondary and tertiary education Indicator 10. Ratio of literate females to males 15-24 years old Indicator 11. Share of women in wage employment in the non-agricultural sector Indicator 12. Proportion of seats held by women in national parliament

Goal 4: Reduce child mortality	
Target 5: Reduce by two thirds, between 1990 and 2015, the under-five mortality rate	Indicator 13. Under-five mortality rate Indicator 14. Infant mortality rate Indicator 15. Proportion of 1-year-old children immunised against measles

Goal 5: Improve maternal health	
Target 6: Reduce by three quarters, between 1990 and 2015, the maternal mortality ratio	Indicator 16. Maternal mortality ratio Indicator 17. Proportion of births attended by skilled health personnel

Goal 6: Combat HIV/AIDS, malaria and other diseases	
Target 7: Have halted by 2015 and begun to reverse the spread of HIV/AIDS	Indicator 18. HIV prevalence among 15-24-year-old pregnant women Indicator 19. Condom use rate of the contraceptive prevalence rate Indicator 20. Number of children orphaned by HIV/AIDS
Target 8: Have halted by 2015 and begun to reverse the incidence of malaria and other major diseases	Indicator 21. Prevalence and death rates associated with malaria Indicator 22. Proportion of population in malaria risk areas using effective malaria prevention and treatment measures Indicator 23. Prevalence and death rates associated with tuberculosis Indicator 24. Proportion of tuberculosis cases detected and cured under DOTS (Directly Observed Treatment Short Course)

The Millennium Development Goals, Targets and Indicators (Goals 7-8)

Goal 7: Ensure environmental sustainability	
Target 9: Integrate the principles of sustainable development into country policies and programmes and reverse the loss of environmental resources	Indicator 25. Proportion of land area covered by forest Indicator 26. Ratio of area protected to maintain biological diversity to surface area Indicator 27. Energy use (metric ton oil equivalent) per $1 GDP (PPP) Indicator 28. Carbon dioxide emissions (per capita) and consumption of ozone-depleting CFCs (ODP tons) Indicator 29. Proportion of population using solid fuels
Target 10: Halve, by 2015, the proportion of people without sustainable access to safe drinking water	Indicator 30. Proportion of population with sustainable access to an improved water source, urban and rural
Target 11: By 2020, to have achieved a significant improvement in the lives of at least 100 million slum dwellers	Indicator 31. Proportion of urban population with access to improved sanitation Indicator 32. Proportion of households with access to secure tenure (owned or rented)
Goal 8: Develop a global partnership for development	
Target 12: Develop further an open, rule-based, predictable, non-discriminatory trading and financial system (includes a commitment to good governance, development, and poverty reduction – both nationally and internationally) Target 13: Address the special needs of the least developed countries (includes: tariff and quota free access for LDC exports; enhanced programme of debt relief for HIPC and cancellation of official bilateral debt; and more generous ODA for countries committed to poverty reduction) Target 14: Address the special needs of landlocked countries and small island developing states (through the Programme of Action for the Sustainable Development of Small Island Developing States and the outcome of the 22nd special session of the General Assembly) Target 15: Deal comprehensively with the debt problems of developing countries through national and international measures in order to make debt sustainable in the long term	*Some of the indicators listed below will be monitored separately for the least developed countries (LDCs), Africa, landlocked countries and small island developing States.* *Official Development Assistance* Indicator 33. Net ODA, total and to LDCs, as percentage of OECD/DAC donors' GNI Indicator 34. Proportion of total bilateral, sector-allocable ODA of OECD/DAC donors to basic social services (basic education, primary health care, nutrition, safe water and sanitation) Indicator 35. Proportion of bilateral ODA of OECD/DAC donors that is untied Indicator 36. ODA received in landlocked countries as proportion of their GNIs Indicator 37. ODA received in small island developing States as proportion of their GNIs *Market Access* Indicator 38. Proportion of total developed country imports (by value and excluding arms) from developing countries and from LDCs, admitted free of duties Indicator 39. Average tariffs imposed by developed countries on agricultural products and textiles and clothing from developing countries Indicator 40. Agricultural support estimate for OECD countries as percentage of their GDP Indicator 41. Proportion of ODA provided to help build trade capacity *Debt Sustainability* Indicator 42. Total number of countries that have reached their HIPC decision points and number that have reached their HIPC completion points (cumulative) Indicator 43. Debt relief committed under HIPC initiative, US$ Indicator 44. Debt service as a percentage of exports of goods and services

The Millennium Development Goals, Targets and Indicators (Goal 8, cont.)

Goal 8: Develop a global partnership for development	
Target 16: In co-operation with developing countries, develop and implement strategies for decent and productive work for youth	Indicator 45. Unemployment rate of 15-to-24-year-olds, each sex and total
Target 17: In co-operation with pharmaceutical companies, provide access to affordable, essential drugs in developing countries	Indicator 46. Proportion of population with access to affordable essential drugs on a sustainable basis
Target 18: In co-operation with the private sector, make available the benefits of new technologies, especially information and communications	Indicator 47. Telephone lines and cellular subscribers per 100 population Indicator 48. Personal computers in use per 100 population and Internet users per 100 population

Appendix C: Data on Development and Democracy in the Commonwealth

1. Population, HDI rank and poverty level

	Pop. (thousands) 2000	HDI Rank 2000	Pop. below poverty line (%) Rural	Pop. below poverty line (%) Urban	Pop. below poverty line (%) National	Pop. below $1/day	Pop. below $2/day
Antigua and Barbuda	68	52					
Australia	19,182	5					
Bahamas, The	303	41					
Bangladesh	131,050	145	39.8	14.3	35.6	29.1	77.8
Barbados	267	31					
Belize	240	58					
Botswana	1,602	126				33.3	61.4
Brunei Darussalam	338	32					
Cameroon	14,876	135	32.4	44.4	40.0	33.4	64.4
Canada	30,750	3					
Cyprus	757	26					
Dominica	73	61					
Fiji Islands	812	72					
Gambia, The	1,303	160			64.0	59.3	82.9
Ghana	19,306	129	34.3	26.7	31.4	44.8	78.5
Grenada	98	83					
Guyana	761	103			43.2		
India	1,015,923	124	36.7	30.5	35.0	44.2	86.2
Jamaica	2,633	86			18.7	3.2	25.2
Kenya	30,092	134	46.4	29.3	42.0	26.5	62.3
Kiribati	91						
Lesotho	2,035	132	53.9	27.8	49.2	43.1	65.7
Malawi	10,311	163			54.0		
Malaysia	23,270	59			15.5		
Maldives	276	84					
Malta	390	30					
Mauritius	1,186	67			10.6		
Mozambique	17,691	170				37.8	78.4
Namibia	1,757	122				34.9	55.8
Nauru	12						
New Zealand	3,831	19					
Nigeria	126,910	148	36.4	30.4	34.1	70.2	90.8
Pakistan	138,080	138	36.9	28.0	34.0	31.0	84.6
Papua New Guinea	5,130	133					
St Kitts and Nevis	41	44					
St Lucia	156	66					
St Vincent and the Grenadines	115	91					
Samoa	170	101					

	Pop. (thousands) 2000	HDI Rank 2000	Pop. below poverty line (%)			Pop. below	
			Rural	Urban	National	$1/day	$2/day
Seychelles	81	47					
Sierra Leone	5,031	173	76.0	53.0	68.0	57.0	74.5
Singapore	4,018	25					
Solomon Islands	447	121					
South Africa	42,801	107				11.5	35.8
Sri Lanka	19,359	89	27.0	15.0	25.0	6.6	45.4
Swaziland	1,045	125			40.0		
Tonga	100						
Trinidad and Tobago	1,301	50	20.0	24.0	21.0	12.4	39.0
Tuvalu	10						
Uganda	22,210	150			55.0		
United Kingdom	59,739	13					
United Republic of Tanzania	33,696	151	49.7	24.4	41.6	19.9	59.6
Vanuatu	197	131					
Zambia	10,089	153			86.0	63.6	87.4
Zimbabwe	12,627	128	31.0	10.0	25.5	36.0	64.2

Sources: Population from World Bank, *World Bank Atlas 2002*, Washington D.C.; population below the poverty line from World Bank, *World Development Report 2003*, Washington D.C.; all other data from UNDP, *Human Development Report 2002*, New York.

2. GNI (GDP), Debt Service and ODA

	GNI (GNP) 2000	Total Debt Service paid 2000	Debt Service as a percentage of GNI 2000	Net Oficial Development Aid or Official Aid 2000
	(million US$)		(%)	(million US$)
Antigua and Barbuda	642			9.8
Australia	388,252			
Bahamas	4,533			5.5
Bangladesh	47,864	790.0	1.7	1,171.5
Barbados	2,469			0.3
Belize	746	66.1	8.9	14.7
Botswana	5,280	68.0	1.3	30.7
Brunei Darussalam	n.a.			0.6
Cameroon	8,644	562.0	6.5	379.9
Canada	649,829			
Cyprus	9,361			54.5
Dominica	233	10.2		15.5
Fiji Islands	1,480	30.1	2.0	29.1
Gambia, The	440	18.6	4.2	49.1
Ghana	6,594	472.0	7.2	609.4
Grenada	370	12.0	3.2	16.5
Guyana	652	116.0	17.8	108.3
India	454,800	9,921.0	2.2	1,487.2
Jamaica	6,883	643.0	9.3	10.0
Kenya	10,610	481.0	4.5	512.3
Kiribati	86			17.9
Lesotho	1,181	65.8	5.6	41.5
Malawi	1,744	59.0	3.4	445.3
Malaysia	78,727	5,967.0	7.6	45.4
Maldives	541	19.9	3.7	19.3
Malta	3,559			21.2
Mauritius	4,449	553.0	12.4	20.5
Mozambique	3,746	88.0	2.3	876.2
Namibia	3,569			151.7
Nauru	n.a.			4.0
New Zealand	49,750			
Nigeria	32,705	1,009.0	3.1	184.8
Pakistan	61,022	2,857.0	4.7	702.8
Papua New Guinea	3,607	305.0	8.5	275.4
St Kitts and Nevis	269	19.6	7.3	3.9
St Lucia	642	40.3	6.3	11.0
St Vincent and the Grenadines	313	15.4	4.9	6.2
Samoa	246	8.5	3.5	27.4

	GNI (GNP) 2000	Total Debt Service paid 2000	Debt Service as a percentage of GNI 2000	Net Oficial Development Aid or Official Aid 2000
	(million US$)		(%)	(million US$)
Seychelles	573	17.4	3.0	18.3
Sierra Leone	647	43.0	6.6	182.4
Singapore	99,404			1.1
Solomon Islands	278	9.1	3.3	68.4
South Africa	129,171	3,860.0	3.0	487.5
Sri Lanka	16,408	738.0	4.5	276.3
Swaziland	1,451	23.6	1.6	13.2
Tonga	166	4.1	2.5	18.8
Trinidad & Tobago	6,415	500.0	7.8	-1.5
Tuvalu	n.a.			4.0
Uganda	6,699	159.0	2.4	819.5
United Kingdom	1,459,500			
United Republic of Tanzania	9,013	217.0	2.4	1,044.6
Vanuatu	226	2.2	1.0	45.8
Zambia	3,026	186.0	6.1	795.1
Zimbabwe	5,851	471.0	8.0	178.1

Sources: GNI (GNP) from World Bank, *World Bank Atlas 2002*, Washington DC; Total Debt Service paid from World Bank, *Global Development Finance 2002*, Washington DC; Net Official Development Assistance from OECD, *Geographical Distribution of Financial Flows to Aid Recipients 2002*, Paris.

3. Political participation

	Participation		Seats in legislature held by women (as % of total)
	Voter turnout (legislative elections)		
	Year	(%)	
Antigua and Barbuda	1999	64	8.3
Australia	2001	95	26.5
Bahamas, The	1997	68	19.6
Bangladesh	2001	75	2.0
Barbados	1999	63	20.4
Belize	1998	90	13.5
Botswana	1999	77	17.0
Brunei Darussalam			
Cameroon	1997	76	5.6
Canada	2000	61	23.6
Cyprus	2001	91	10.7
Dominica	2000	60	18.8
Fiji Islands	2001	78	
Gambia, The	2002	69	2.0
Ghana	2000	62	9.0
Grenada	1999	57	17.9
Guyana	2001	89	20.0
India	1999	60	8.9
Jamaica	1997	65	16.0
Kenya	1997	65	3.6
Kiribati			
Lesotho	1998	74	10.7
Malawi	1999	92	9.3
Malaysia	1999		14.5
Maldives	1999	74	6.0
Malta	1998	95	9.2
Mauritius	2000	81	5.7
Mozambique	1999	80	30.0
Namibia	1999	63	20.4
Nauru			
New Zealand	1999	90	30.8
Nigeria	1999	41	3.3
Pakistan	1997	35	
Papua New Guinea	1997	81	1.8
St Kitts and Nevis	2000	64	13.3
St Lucia	2001	53	13.8
St Vincent and the Grenadines	2001	69	22.7
Samoa	2001	86	6.1

	Participation		
	Voter turnout (legislative elections)		Seats in legislature held by women (as % of total)
	Year	(%)	
Seychelles	1998	87	23.5
Sierra Leone	1996	50	8.8
Singapore	2001	95	11.8
Solomon Islands	2001	62	0.0
South Africa	1999	89	29.8
Sri Lanka	2001	80	4.4
Swaziland	1998		6.3
Tonga			
Trinidad and Tobago	2001	62	20.9
Tuvalu			
Uganda	2001	70	24.7
United Kingdom	2001	59	17.1
United Republic of Tanzania	2000	84	22.3
Vanuatu	1998	75	0.0
Zambia	2001	68	12.0
Zimbabwe	2000	49	10.0

Source: UNDP, *Human Development Report 2002*, New York.

Appendix D: Members of the Commonwealth Expert Group on Development and Democracy

Dr Manmohan Singh (India) – Chairman – is currently the Leader of the Opposition, Rajya Sabha (Council of States), Parliament of India. He has previously served in many other positions of the Indian Government, including Finance Minister, Adviser to the Prime Minister of India on Economic Affairs, Secretary Ministry of Finance, Governor of the Reserve Bank of India, Deputy Chairman of the Indian Planning Commission and Chief Economic Adviser to India's Ministry of Finance. He gained the 1993 Euromoncy Award for Finance Minister of the Year and twice received the Asiamoney Award for Finance Minister of the Year (1993, 1994). Dr. Singh has received a number of other awards and has been presented with honorary degrees from institutions all over the world.

Hon Jocelyne Bourgon (Canada) has had a distinguished career in the Canadian public service. She was the first woman to be appointed Clerk of the Privy Council and Secretary to the Cabinet. From 1994-99, Ms Bourgon led the Public Service of Canada through some of its most important reforms since the 1940s. She has also served as the President of the Canadian Centre for Management Development and is an active member of various international boards and advisory committees. In 1998, Ms Bourgon was summoned to the Queen's Privy Council for Canada in recognition of her contribution to her country. She is currently Canada's Ambassador to the Organisation for Economic Co-operation and Development (OECD).

Mr Robert Champion de Crespigny AC (Australia) is a businessman operating in a number of capacities from his office based in Adelaide, South Australia. He is Chairman of the Economic Development Board of South Australia, an Advisory Board created by Premier Mike Rann in April 2002, charged with the responsibility of delivering recommendations and overseeing the implementation of changes to the South Australian economy. He is also Chairman and member of several professional, business and charitable organisations.

Sir Richard Jolly (UK) has had an outstanding career as an academic and international civil servant. He is Honorary Professor and Research Associate of the Institute of Development Studies (IDS) at the University of Sussex. He was previously Director of IDS. Sir Richard has also been an Assistant Secretary-General of the United Nations, serving as Deputy Executive Director of the United Nations Children's Fund (UNICEF) and subsequently as senior adviser to the Administrator of the United Nations Development Programme (UNDP). In the latter capacity he was co-ordinator of the widely acclaimed *Human Development Report*.

Mr Martin Khor (Malaysia) is the Director of the International Secretariat of the Third World Network. He was also a Member of the Board of the South Centre (1996-

2002) and formerly a Vice Chairman of the Expert Group on the Right to Development of the UN Commission on Human Rights. He is also a member of and Consultant to the Consultative Group on Globalisation established under the National Economic Action Council in the Prime Minister's Department in Malaysia. In addition, he has been a Consultant to the United Nations Conference on Trade and Development (UNCTAD), UNDP, United Nations Environment Programme (UNEP) and the UN University, and has conducted studies and written papers for these agencies. Mr Khor has written several books and papers on trade and World Trade Organisation (WTO) issues, and on environment and development.

Prof Akinjide Osuntokun (Nigeria) holds a BA Degree in History from the University of Ibadan and a PhD from Dalhousie University, Canada. He had taught in the Universities in Barbados, Lagos, Jos and Maduguri. He was the Director of Nigeria Universities Office in the US and Canada. He was appointed in 1988 as Special Adviser to the Minister of Foreign Affairs in Nigeria and from 1991-1995 he was Nigeria's Ambassador to Germany. He returned to Nigeria in 1995 and was appointed Head of the Department of History, University of Lagos, and he is currently a member of the Advisory Council on Foreign Affairs to President Obassanjo.

Dr Salim Ahmed Salim (Tanzania) has held high-level positions at both the national and international levels. He has held key posts in the Government of the United Republic of Tanzania, including Prime Minister. Dr Salim was also Secretary-General of the Organisation of African Unity for an unprecedented three terms. When he was Tanzania's Permanent Representative to the United Nations, in New York, he was elected as President of the Security Council as well as the General Assembly. Dr Salim has chaired several international committees and conferences and holds a number of honours and decorations.

H E Tuiloma Neroni Slade (Samoa) was, at the time of the work of the Expert Group, the Permanent Representative of Samoa to the United Nations. A former Attorney General of Samoa, he is now a Judge of the International Criminal Court in The Hague, The Netherlands.

Sir Dwight Venner (St Lucia) is currently Governor of the Eastern Caribbean Central Bank, a position he has held since December 1989. Prior to that he served in the position of Director of Financial Planning in the St Lucian Government. Sir Dwight has written and published extensively in the areas of Monetary and International Economics, Central Banking, Public Finance, Economic Development, Political Economy and International Economic Relations. Sir Dwight was awarded Commander of the British Empire (CBE) in 1996 in St Lucia. In June 2001, he was awarded Knight Commander of the Most Excellent Order of the British Empire (KBE) in St Vincent and the Grenadines for services to the financial sector.

Dr Ngaire Woods (New Zealand) is Director of the Global Economy Governance